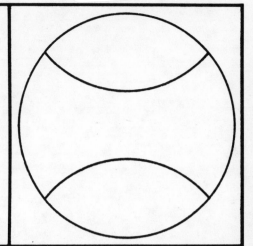

Peter Burwash's
Tennis
for
Life

Confidence Comes With
Demonstrated Ability

Pain Is Temporary
Victory Is Forever

Peter Burwash's *Tennis for Life*

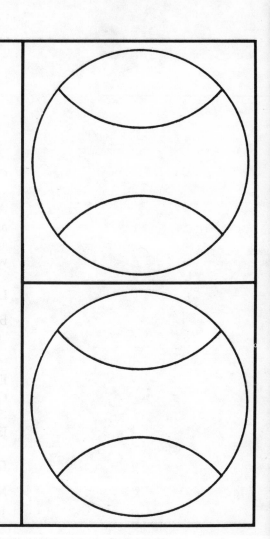

by
Peter Burwash
and
John Tullius

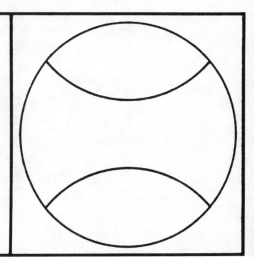

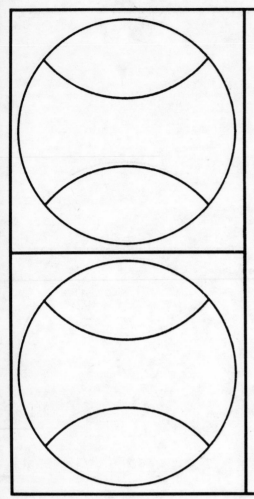

Library of Congress Cataloging in Publication Data

Burwash, Peter.
  Peter Burwash's Tennis for life.

  1. Tennis.   I. Tullius, John.   II. Title.
III. Title: Tennis for life.
GV995.B84   1980   796.342′2   80-50767
ISBN 0-8129-0952-6 (hardcover)
ISBN 0-8129-6322-9 (paper)

Designed by Sam Gantt

Manufactured in the United States of America
10 9 8 7 6 5 4 3 2 1

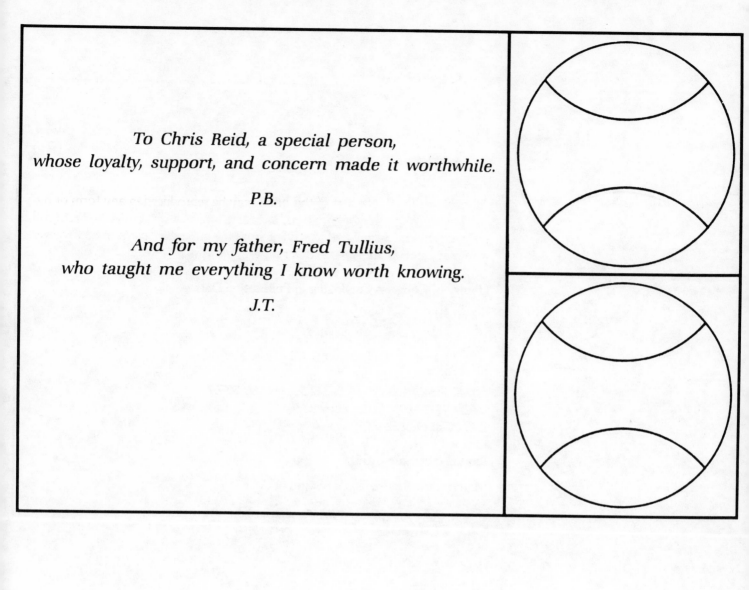

To Chris Reid, a special person,
whose loyalty, support, and concern made it worthwhile.

P.B.

And for my father, Fred Tullius,
who taught me everything I know worth knowing.

J.T.

Acknowledgments

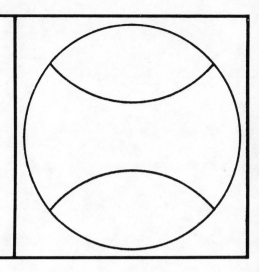

To my mother and father, for always giving and caring.

To Bruce Haase, for his incredible energy in personally taking and developing almost all of the photos in the book.

To Chris Reid, for her patient and detailed work on the manuscript.

To Rob Smith, Bernard Gusman, Karen Kruse, Monika Dinhoffer, Sue Aubuchon, Jim Martinez, and Shannon Robinson, for their behind-the-scenes efforts in getting the manuscript typed and put together.

To Bob Gillen and Barry Tarshis, for their guidance and concern.

To Larry Huebner, one of the few people who believed in me in the beginning.

To Don Goodwin, whose foresight helped create PBI.

To Ben Wise, who gave me the opportunity to start the concept of PBI.

To Joe Dinhoffer for his tremendous efforts and support.

Finally, to all the PBI professionals, for their loyal support in seeing the book become a reality.

Contents

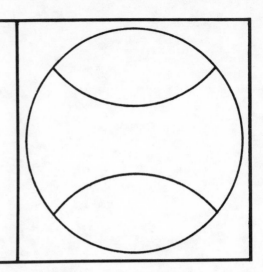

PHASE THREE—HOW TO BE YOUR OWN COACH
PART II: SIMPLICITY CHECKPOINTS

PHASE FOUR—UNDERSTANDING STRATEGY

PHASE FIVE—A GUIDE FOR THE HEALTH-CONSCIOUS TENNIS PLAYER

Introduction
The Peter Burwash Story
by John Tullius

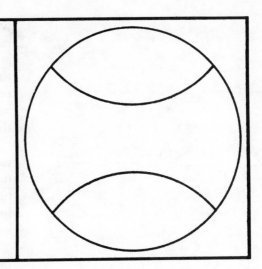

The first time I ever saw Peter Burwash he was sprawled flat on his stomach on a tennis court. He got up with blood trickling down his leg and brushed himself off. On the next point he dove for a wide shot, rolled and hit the fence, got up, dove again, got up, and hit a winner. The crowd cheered but didn't exactly lose its mind. Personally, I had lost mine—my jaw was down to my knees. But as I was to learn, this display of unbelievable guts and hustle was Peter's "style." No big deal—he does it all the time.

That's the way Peter Burwash plays tennis and the way, in fact, that he lives his entire life—with an unbelievable ferocity and energy. After traveling around the world playing tennis, following the circuit, writing articles for several tennis publications (*Tennis, Tennis USA,* etc.), and meeting everyone from Jimmy Connors to Bud Collins, I was still most impressed with Peter Burwash. In fact, it wasn't even close. But this is not the chronicle of a great champion—though Peter was a two-time Canadian Davis Cup player and the number-one player in Canada in 1971, and won a remarkable nineteen international titles. Rather, this is the story of a very rare species in life—a man who not only has fulfilled his potential, but has surpassed it.

Like most beginnings, the beginning of Peter Burwash's tennis career starts before the start—on a hockey rink. Born in Ontario, Canada, he eventually played left wing for the University of Toronto on a team considered to be one of the strongest collegiate teams of all time. Almost the entire team received professional offers, and when Peter himself was drafted into the National Hockey League by the St. Louis Blues a lifelong dream was fulfilled. He now had several weeks to prepare himself, and he went about his practice the way he went about everything—with a fury. He chased down all pucks, checked and skated as if he were in the Stanley Cup playoffs, and perhaps this extra little bit of competitive madness was what opened the door to a new life.

Most of us encounter some crucial event in our lives that opens our eyes, turns us around, and puts us on a new path. For Peter the door that opened was a penalty-box door left slightly ajar. He was checked and his spine was rammed at breakneck speed into the edge of the door. They skated on around him for a couple of minutes until they realized that he was not going to get up. He was completely paralyzed from the waist down. They stuck pins in his feet and legs and he felt nothing. He would recover in an hour or so, but at that moment he was very, very scared. Not surprisingly, what went through his mind was the brutality of hockey.

"I remember one time I was skating down the ice and my best friend was next to me and he took a puck in the mouth and lost all of his teeth, up and down, right back to the molars in one whack. Didn't knock them out, really, just sheared them off right at the gums. Fortunately, I only lost seven or eight teeth. I was one of the few guys who didn't take his teeth out and put them in a cup at night.

"The whole time I was lying there I just went over the entire thing in my mind and I thought, 'If I ever walk away from this it will be the last hockey I'll ever play.' I'd had enough of the bitter-cold climates and the brutality, but most of all I'd fulfilled all my goals in hockey. I needed a new challenge."

In a short while the feeling returned to his legs, and when he got back to his apartment a couple of hours later he phoned the organizer of a small Florida tennis circuit, talked his way into an opening, grabbed his coat, shut off the light, and drove to his parents' home to pick up his racquets and a suitcase of clothes and become a tennis player. There was only one minor problem—his parents lived in Toronto, 3,200 miles away!

He drove 3,200 miles in the dead of winter in three days without sleep, caught a plane to Miami on the fourth day, and got to the quarters of a tournament in West Palm Beach. A couple more phone calls and two days later he flew to London, took a train to Nice, then hitchhiked to Monte Carlo, where he was supposed to play the next morning in a tournament which was part of the famous French Riviera circuit. He had $300 in his pocket and no return ticket, and he planned to stay in Europe right on through to Wimbledon five months later. After travel expenses, his budget worked out to fifteen cents a day for meals. That did not, however, include money for shoes, clothing, toothpaste, razor blades—or a room to sleep in. But who needs a room when last week you were paralyzed and now you're a touring professional tennis player? Peter was flying. Heck, he'd sleep on a cloud.

The Monte Carlo Country Club, in a word, has class. The clubhouse overlooks the entire French Riviera, with white cliffs jutting right up out of the Mediterranean, and below you are immaculately groomed red clay courts banked against that sunshine blue sky.

"I walked out there that first day, and I was so thrilled to be playing in my first international tournament. I was so high! So I hurried over to look at the draw to see who I was playing and my first-round opponent turns out to be Ray Antignant, who I find out is forty-seven years old! And here I am twenty-two, twenty-three, at the time, and I think to myself, 'This is absolutely fantastic! I get to play an old man.' And I walk out there at twelve o'clock sharp and I'm on the pro circuit at maybe the classiest club in the world and I'm gonna get by the first round. No question! So at six-thirty, six and a half hours later, I walked off the court! I beat him 22–20, 8–6. That was my first taste of Europe."

The circuit that Peter jumped into was one of the toughest tests of survival ever devised for a tennis player. It was filled with the great clay-court players

Peter winning the Canada Games Gold Medal Singles title in Burnaby, British Columbia, Canada, in August 1973. (Photo courtesy of Prière de Mentionner.)

at a time when clay-court tennis was at its zenith. Players like Ilie Nastase, Ion Tiriac, Jan Kodes, Onny Parun, Vladimir Zednick, Cliff Richey, Frantisek Pala—some of the finest players to step foot on a clay court.

And in those transitional years of the late '60s, between "Shamateurism" and open tennis, there wasn't even decent prize money to ease the struggle. If you won a tournament you might get $75 or $100. And with so many great players it was a ditch battle to get as far as the quarters and win $20.

"It was a desperate time just to stay on the circuit. But once you were out there you were hooked. It was like *Catch-22*. You had just enough money to

"The Flying Canadian," in December 1968.

get to the next tourney but not enough to go home. So you had to keep going until you won enough money to quit but if you were doing that well—why quit?

"Players would do anything to get by. Some lived in tents, some in the back seats of their cars. They strung racquets, gave lessons, and umpired matches. But probably the most lucrative pastime was the selling of equipment. Guys would fly into a country and fly out with nothing. They sold everything—strings, frames, shoes, shirts. They'd bring their entire suitcase into a club and they'd go home empty. Sometimes they'd even sell the suitcase."

After Monte Carlo it was all downhill on the French Riviera. The tour went next to Juan-les-Pins, then Villareuse, Menton, Beaulieu, Cannes, Nice. At Juan-les-Pins, a tiny three-court club with one cold-water shower and a shack for a locker room, they claimed they had not received his entry. "I found out later that anything written in English they threw out. I finally talked my way in, but I had no room, no meals, no entry. I was under the assumption that as long as I got on the circuit everything would be okay."

But everything was definitely not "okay." First of all, though Peter had won the Canadian Collegiate Championships three straight years, it was not exactly the most difficult title to win. He would take four days off from hockey practice to tune up, spend three days winning the tournament, and then back to the ice. His only real "win" was against Canada's number-two player at the time, Harry Fauquier. And when he showed up on the French Riviera thinking all would be okay, that was the only player of any significance he'd ever beaten. That was his entire tournament record—Harry Fauquier!

And, secondly, on a budget of fifteen cents a day, playing anywhere from five to fifteen sets of grueling clay-court tennis, it boggles even the penny-pinchingest mind how he managed to stay alive.

"I have great memories of buying my loaf of day-old French bread for twelve cents and carrying that home and marking off with a knife what I'd be able to have each day for the next five days. And I had my jar of peanut butter. I would analyze my expenditures for eight weeks so I'd figure nine cents for peanut butter and so on. That's what I'd guaranteed myself—French bread and peanut butter. And then I had my glucose tablets. You could get a big jar for a dollar, because all they are is sugar. But I needed those—I needed energy to practice because I was always losing in the first or second round.

"Then Nastase and Tiriac used to give me the scraps off their plates. They were on the Rumanian Tennis Federation expense account, and so they'd order extras and give it to me. I don't care what they say about him, if it wasn't for Nastase I would have starved to death. So I'd have a peanut-butter sandwich and a glucose tablet for breakfast, a glucose tablet at lunch, and then Nastase would take care of me at dinner."

Finding a room was no less difficult a problem. In one tournament he slept in the clubhouse on two folding chairs placed side by side. The next morning he couldn't lift his arm high enough to serve. So he asked around and finally three Polish Davis Cup players allowed him to sleep on the cement floor of their tiny room in his track suit, with his shoes and tennis shorts for a pillow. After that, Peter would do anything for a room and he became a sort of laundry service for the players who would let him sleep on their floor.

Although Peter was not blessed with great talent, he had a great heart. He would do anything to get the ball back over the net. He dove on concrete, climbed fences, and ran and ran and ran. Because of years of these headlong dives his elbows are piles of bone chips and his legs are heavily scarred. He became known eventually as the "Flying Canadian," and every time he's played he's lived up to that name.

But he was competing with the best that first winter on the French Riviera, and after a couple months of scraping and hustling on and off the court, Peter was broke. But really *broke!* He had managed to use every trick possible to stay on the circuit, but he had reached the end of the line when he walked into the tiny Italian village of Reggio Calabria.

"It was six A.M. when I walked into town. The club was locked up, so I climbed over the wall, because I was very anxious to see what my draw was. If I didn't do well there I was going to have to give up tennis. I had no money. I'd spent every last penny just to get there. So I check the draw—first round, center court, Cliff Richey. One of the best clay-court players ever.

"Picture it. I was a hockey player four months before and I'm at this tournament in this tiny off-the-map village called Reggio Calabria, where they've got two red clay courts and everybody's there—Riessen, Alexander, Newcombe, Dent. And I've got to play Richey in the first round."

Peter played, as he described it, "the best match of my life." But after three and a half hours of grueling tennis, covered head to toe in red clay, bleeding from several headlong slides and completely drained, he came up short—11–9 in the third set. This was the end of his tennis career. What it all came down to was a great loss to a very good player.

"It was one of those unbelievable matches in which two determined players face each other, only one was a lot better than the other. It was on the main court, and a huge crowd gathered as word spread of a good match. Before it was over everybody in Reggio Calabria was there."

The crowd gave the players a long, long ovation for a wonderful display of courage, and then Peter went into the locker room and sat for an hour wondering what he would do, completely broke, the end of the line in a small village in Italy, 8,000 miles from home. When he finally packed it in and

PBI's prison program. Here, Bruce Haase (third from the left) directs the program at the Hawaii State Prison. This program began in 1975 and twice a week a PBI professional goes in to teach.

went into the clubhouse to give his final farewells, he was informed that because of "the most unbelievable performance of courage ever seen at Reggio Calabria" (that's the way the papers put it the next day), Peter was awarded an unheard-of $80 by the Italian Tennis Federation.

He was still alive.

"That money got me to Stuttgart, to Wiesbaden, to Baden-Baden, to Leverkusen—the German circuit. And from there, with the added confidence and experience I was gaining, I made it all the way through the summer to Wimbledon.

"When I got back home, three Canadians—Issy Sharp, Eddie Creed, and Murray Koffler—gave me thirty-five hundred dollars to play the following year. If I owe my career to anything it's to my guts and those three guys. I never became a great player and I never had any illusions about it. I just tried as hard as I could."

The founding of Peter Burwash International (PBI), the world's first international network of traveling tennis coaches, was no less a struggle for Peter. When he first attempted to put PBI together, he contacted hundreds of hotel and resort owners and they all told him his concepts simply would not work. Six years later he heads the largest international group of tennis professionals, staffing many of the world's finest resorts, hotels, clubs, and camps on five continents—from Malaysia to Martinique, in Hawaii, Los Angeles, Tokyo, Dubai, and Munich.

Peter developed the concept of PBI several years ago when he was ranked number three in Canada and competition had become so fierce that he found it difficult to get into tournaments.

"There are so many good players who have no place to go. PBI helps a lot of people stay in tennis. But our professionals are chosen primarily because of their personal strengths, not only because they play a good game of tennis. I concentrated on hiring quality human beings, not just quality tennis players. And that's the real secret of PBI's success. I get hundreds of letters a year from students who say, 'What a fantastic individual, I learned so much!' A fifty-year-old chairman of the the board writing me about what he learned about life from a twenty-two-year-old kid. To me that is the real success of PBI."

The selection and training of a PBI pro is rigorous. Each pro is handpicked from thousands of applicants and then they are trained 420 hours before they can teach their first hour of tennis. Training includes typing, racquet stringing, handling a 35mm camera, and developing black-and-white film. The pros also have courses in accounting, public relations, pro-shop administration, communications, the travel industry, and court construction and maintenance. They must also be bilingual within six to twelve months and trilingual in two years after joining PBI. One PBI pro can already teach tennis in four languages.

Ted Murray working with PBI's wheelchair program in Honolulu, where the world-wide program for handicapped players began.

Though the staffing of resorts is PBI's principal function, the glamour positions are the touring pros of the PBI Traveling Tennis Show. The "Show" is ninety minutes of first-rate entertainment and instruction, which has been described as the Harlem Globetrotters of tennis. So far Peter has given over 5,000 shows and clinics in eighty-six countries, all fifty states, and every Canadian province—to Malawi, East Africa, in a single-engine plane where Peter rigged a court right on the runway; to Micronesia in the Pacific, where the natives played barebreasted; to Tokyo, for a special performance on the Emperor of Japan's birthday before 3,000 people in the National Stadium.

The real heart of PBI, however, is its special programs. PBI now has special programs for children under three, for the blind and the deaf, and for the physically and mentally handicapped, and a nationwide prison program. The idea for the special programs was developed during Peter's trips to Southeast Asia during the Vietnam War.

"While I was in Vietnam I visited a lot of hospitals. Land mines are very prevalent in guerrilla wars, so there were a lot of guys who'd lost legs. But I still remember most vividly the double-amputee ward. There wasn't a leg in the place. There were about a dozen guys there, and I gave a group a tennis lesson, and sometimes it was quite painful because some of them had just lost their legs, but they loved it so much, pain wasn't going to stop them.

"We cleared the beds along the sides and corners and we had this huge cement floor, so we were able to have a very good tennis lesson, because I got down and volleyed and ground-stroked with them right on the floor. I hear people say, 'If I lost an eye I wouldn't want to live.' Well, I saw guys who'd lost both legs and arms and never gave up the hope of living.

"And that instilled something in me. I got the idea I wanted to bring tennis to all those people who had never had the chance to experience tennis before—to every corner of the world, to all those in wheelchairs, to the deaf and the blind. And even those in prisons."

Perhaps the person who knows best the positive effect of PBI's prison program is Billy Johnson. Billy is the tennis champ at the Hawaii State Prison on Oahu. He started playing four years ago after Peter introduced tennis to the inmates—set up a court and net and brought in balls and racquets. But Billy didn't go for the idea right off.

"When Peter first came in I look at this little shrimp and think, 'Who the hell are you?' I was a totally negative person. I'd do anything to give resistance. I used to eat downs, push dope when I was twelve, thirteen—committed four robberies. I been in the slam since twelve. I was one straight year in solitary. Even escaped for eight hours. They had a thing in the paper in Honolulu said I was one of the ten most dangerous prisoners in the state. I was all negative—no positive. That was before tennis.

"Peter came in and did the 'fire drill' where he lines four guys up against the wall and fires balls at them as hard as he can hit 'em. You gotta have courage to hit at those prison guys. You got murderers, rapers—to hit balls at them takes courage. Peter talks with the cons here like he's one of the boys. He's got a mean aura—when he goes by a group of people if they're negative they're gonna change positive.

"Peter is a giver. As long as you know he's in your corner you're all right. Before Peter came here I didn't know if I was gonna get up the next day. Now I gotta get up to play tennis. I wanna get up. I'm excited!

"I made a lot of changes for myself through tennis. I'm totally into health now—I used to weigh two hundred and seventy pounds, now I'm one-ninety. I jump rope, do calisthenics, run a mile. And I'm totally off drugs now. You can't think straight to play tennis if you're drugging it.

"I been in here nine years, and tennis is the first positive thing in my life. I love tennis—really love it. My heart beats faster when I think about it. It's my peace of mind in here. I do my time, but I do my time thinking tennis." Suddenly, Billy gets a far-off look, then smiles and says, "They call Peter the Flyin' Canadian. I wanna be the Flyin' Hawaiian."

On July 18, 1979, through the help of Peter Burwash, Billy Johnson was released from the Hawaii State Prison. He plays tennis every day.

Phase One
Understanding the Game

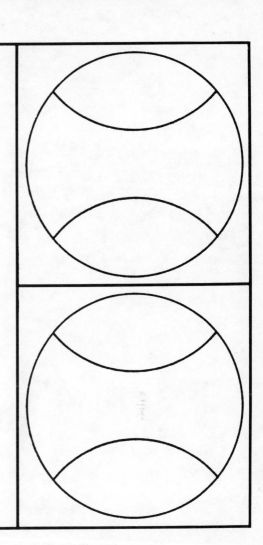

Chapter One
Getting Unstuck

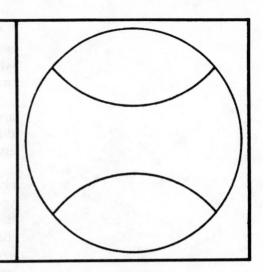

If you're like almost every other tennis player, you've reached a plateau on which you're stuck. No matter how hard you practice, no matter how many lessons you take, you're stuck on that level. Most likely it's that intermediate level of the typical club player, somewhere near the top of the C or B ladder. But you're not good enough for the A's or to play in local open tournaments.

You probably really tried for a while to get better. You went to a few pros in town, and they all corrected your stroke "flaw." And that was guaranteed to put you on that mythical A level. But it never did. That's where a significant number in the tennis teaching profession have let students and players down. Many pros give beginning and intermediate lessons but they can never seem to get you past that intermediate level. Once you get the ball over the net, you're more or less on your own. So after five years of frustration you probably gave up. You figured, "That's it! I guess I've reached my potential—the eternal C player relegated to the same old boring doubles match every weekend."

Well, there is a way to get *unstuck!* No matter what level you're on, from beginner to tournament player, you can start improving immediately by gaining an overall *understanding* of tennis.

We've all seen lessons where a pro stands next to his shopping cart and feeds balls to a student and corrects any "flaws" in his forehand or backhand. But where and when does a player hit those strokes? And for what reasons?

A lesson is often a highly segregated hour so divorced from the game of tennis that you have trouble ever using what you learn. A pro will try to teach you the "perfect" backhand, which the pro himself may admit takes years (and years) to master. Even though it may be a "classic stroke" designed to really pulverize the ball, you usually give up and go back to your old ways, because what the pro is teaching you just doesn't apply to your game for a good five years. The lesson, then, may be totally useless. It's as if you asked me directions to Chicago and I gave you a map of Chicago itself. Nice, but useless until you get there.

It's like being given one piece of a jigsaw puzzle and being expected to know what the puzzle looks like. That's why you're given a picture of the completed puzzle on the box—so you can see the overall picture. You may not be able to fit the piece right into the puzzle, but you've got a pretty good idea where it goes.

That's what I want to do—show you the entire picture right from the beginning so you can piece it together that much faster. So you can see where you are and where you're going and plot out a plan for your improvement.

You must see the entire picture if you want to get to the next level. There are so many variables in the game of tennis—different climatic conditions, different spins, different surfaces, different balls—that you must become aware of them all in order to understand what is holding you back.

You may believe you're suffering from snakebite, but if you actually have cholera, all the antivenin in the world is not going to help you. You may think your lousy backhand has been your problem all along, but it may be that you have horrible court positioning and you're forced to run a mile to even get to that backhand. Simply understanding court positioning may catapult you over an opponent you have never beaten—overnight. Now wouldn't that be nice?

I've organized the understanding of the game into a five-phase program. Phase One, "Understanding the Game," is a basic overall view of the game that orients you to the primarily defensive nature of tennis and introduces you to the three foundations of the game: court awareness, ball awareness, and opponent awareness. Phases Two and Three, "How to Be Your Own Coach," (part one and part two) show you how to develop solid, effective strokes that will suit *your* game and *your* ability, while avoiding any emphasis on "classic" form, because one of my strongest beliefs is that there is no one "right" way to hit a ball—only what works. Phase Four, "Understanding Strategy," shows you how, where, and when to hit every shot in every circumstance—including how to exploit your opponent's weaknesses, how to beat a better player, and how to play the big points. Phase Five, "A Guide for the Health-conscious Tennis Player," suggests a strategy for good health that will improve your game because a good tennis player is by necessity a healthy human being.

After you read this book you can go out and play and, probably, for the first time in your tennis career, get an inkling of what's really happening on the court. Then, if you're smart, you will come back to the book, read some more, and go out and experience and experiment. I guarantee that if you do this, in three to six months you will have revolutionized not only your game, but what you understand about the game of tennis. You may, in fact, be really seeing tennis for the first time.

If you want to drive to Chicago you get out a road map. You form an idea of how to get there. You don't just drive out of your driveway and take any old street that you see. You know where you're going or you don't get there. I will show you how an understanding of the game will lead you from your present level to become a better, more self-reliant player—in other words, I'll show you how to be your own coach.

Most instructors start with the teaching of "classic form" because they think it's one of the foundations of the game—the natural place to start building a good tennis game. But "classic" form is really just a preconceived idea of what someone should *look* like while hitting the ball. Form is not a fundamental at all—it's style, and like all styles it changes with time.

Form is nothing more than what the great players over the years found practical. Then, of course, the rest of the tennis population copies the champions, and five to ten years later everybody's got an "Evert backhand." Or to be more accurate, their backhands are in the same style as Evert's.

The point is, form did not come first. Stroke production is a matter of style, and style is secondary to function, to what actually works. When the score goes up it says 6–2, 6–1. Period. It doesn't say "6–2, 6–1, but Chris sure had a nice-looking backhand." *Looking good doesn't win matches.*

The big problem with emphasizing form as the basic foundation for learning tennis is that most instruction deals with what happens in ideal situations. Sometimes a pro will stick you right on top of the net and feed you setups and you bang them straight down into the court for so-called winners. And that's supposed to teach you the volley! Or for forehands he tosses you balls and tells you to get your body sideways, keep your racquet low, and turn your feet this way or that way—which is fine if your opponents would only cooperate. But how many times in a match does that ideal situation come up? Almost never! So he's teaching you a part of the game that you'll almost never use unless you're totally dominating an opponent. And if you're totally dominating a match, heck, you can do anything you want.

I'm not saying not to develop good strokes, because in the long run a superior stroking ability will create powerful, effective ground strokes. In Phase Two, "How to Be Your Own Coach," I'll show you how to develop strokes through the use of "simplicity checkpoints" for each stroke, so that if something goes wrong (for example, you're hitting the back fence on your backhand) you can adjust right then and there. You can give yourself corrective lessons right in the middle of a match.

My point is that stroke production comes a long way down the road and is integrated naturally into your game as you *play*. But there is a much more important emphasis necessary to become a better tennis player, and it isn't to learn perfect strokes or free your mind or become one with the ball. The intention of this book is to teach a player from the beginning an overall awareness, an understanding, of the game, because without understanding you'll be stuck on that plateau forever.

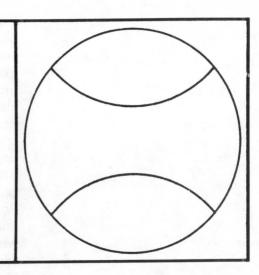

Chapter Two
Common-sense Tennis

1. TENNIS IS A GAME OF EMERGENCIES

To understand tennis, then, is not to learn form, but instead to understand what to do in a match and when to do it. It's the ability to use common sense, to do what's practical under fire—not to memorize a textbook. And most of all, common-sense tennis is the fundamental understanding that tennis is a game of *emergencies.*

Most pros show you the accelerator and the radio and say, "Take off!" They've forgotten all about the brakes! They teach as if tennis were played on a freeway in which everyone gets out of your way no matter what you do. Now, does that sound like *your* last match? If it does, then you've got to stop playing the old lady next door. Because if you're playing someone on your level then he'll probably be putting you into trouble, into one emergency situation after another. And if you play up a level or two there will be a siren going off in your brain almost constantly.

When I played Arthur Ashe at the U.S. Open for the first time I was on a pretty good winning streak. I had been on the international pro circuit for a time and I was consistently getting to the quarters and I even had a few championships under my belt. I knew Ashe was a great player, but I was confident as we were warming up that if I could just get my game going I'd give him a tough go.

But I'd never yet played anyone of Ashe's caliber (he was in his prime and ranked number two in the world), and after the first point I knew I was in over my head. It wasn't just that everything I hit came back, but that every ball Ashe hit put me in trouble. I'd hit my serve and after that I was immediately in trouble. It was the first time I had experienced such constant, intense pressure during a match. Every shot was an emergency situation.

When the car goes out of control, that's an emergency. When your game falls apart during a match, that's an emergency. How do you deal with that? If someone hasn't shown you how to downshift or use the brake, how will you know what to do?

Everything doesn't always go according to plan out on the court. If you're a beginner the ball may get behind you because you were slow off the mark or you reacted late. But a pro will react on time and the ball may still get behind him. Why? Because his opponent created an emergency situation, put him under pressure. In fact, the better player you become, the more emergencies become relevant—because when you challenge better players they have the potential to put you in more trouble. People ask me why I run around like crazy all the time. Because I'm usually playing guys who can put me under pressure.

Everyone meets his match. There are only a few players in the world who can put Connors in trouble. But it happens to everybody. If it happens to Connors it will happen to you. So if players at that level meet their match, imagine how often you'll meet yours. There will come many times in a match when you're totally out of control—you can't get set, you can't get depth, you can't get prepared, you're one step behind, always struggling. Why worry about learning how to set up to hit an ideal forehand when you'll only get that opportunity 10 percent of the time? Why not learn to deal with emergency situations?

In life, if you don't understand how to make things better, you will always be frustrated. That's why a lot of tennis players have quit. They don't know how to get better. To improve in tennis you've got to have a *defensive foundation*.

One problem many players have, however, is accepting the fact that they're on the defensive. Their attitude is, 'I'm going to make an offensive shot no matter what.' Their opponent has just crunched a volley to the corner and they are running like a maniac just to get it. And they try a topspin passing shot that they've never even made in *practice*. And they expect to win matches!

And that's when players run into trouble—not accepting the fact of being on defense. Returning serve, for example, often means being on defense. If you're up against a great serve, the chances are limited that you will get out of that defensive position on one shot. So you've got to understand that, accept it, and try to do something on the next shot.

2. MINIMUM POTENTIAL

There are a thousand things that can go wrong in a match. The ball can take a bad bounce, or hit a line and skid, or you may simply judge the ball poorly. You can never really be sure what will happen next on the court. So you need a "backup" in order to get the ball over when things go wrong. That backup, that ace in the hole, that little bit of stroke insurance, is *minimum potential*.

Minimum potential is simply the understanding that a racquet possesses in its strings a great potential for power *without swinging*. If you're forced into an emergency situation because you're on the run, or the ball is blasted at you, or the wind whips the ball off course, you don't have time for a big swing. Just stick your racquet out with the strings pointing in the direction you want the ball to go and the minimum potential, the natural rebound of the ball off the strings, will supply almost all of the power you'll need.

Remember, the court is only seventy-eight feet long and the ball weighs only about two ounces, so you need only a minimum of effort to hit the ball over the net. In baseball, you can hit a home run. In golf, a long drive is often a bonus. But in tennis, there's no reward for hitting the ball a long way. If you understand minimum potential, you realize that no swing at all is necessary or even desirable on many shots. All you really have time to do in many situations is present your racquet face to the ball and try to get it back over the net. Your opponent often supplies the power and you use your opponent's pace to your advantage.

Chapter Three
The Three Foundations of Tennis:
The Court, the Ball, and the Opponent

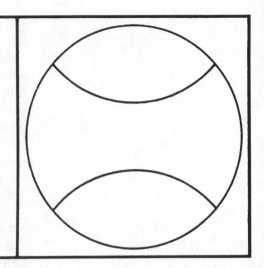

1. DEVELOPING TRIPLE VISION

In all my years of teaching tennis I have never told a student, "Watch the ball!" "Watch the ball" is the most overworked cliche in tennis. But not only is it a cliche, it is also incorrect! Most tennis players are so worried about watching the ball that they've got tunnel vision. Their minds are zeroed in on that little space where the ideal ball is supposed to be hit.

But let's use some common sense. There are three foundations, three necessary elements to the game of tennis—a ball, a court, and an opponent. To play a good game of tennis you must learn to focus on all three of these elements and develop what I call *triple vision*.

A good driver is continually looking in the rear-view and side-view mirrors and yet continues to drive straight ahead, because he has taken a visual image of what's in front of him. In other words, he's using triple vision. The same idea applies in tennis. You should have a visual picture of the court and your opponent at all times. You don't have to constantly look at the ball to know where it is. Most of the time a watch-the-ball addict has no idea where his opponent is or where the potential openings on the court are. His head is down, all his attention's on the ball, and suddenly his opponent sneaks to the net, and the first time he suspects anything's wrong is when he sees the ball hit the other guy's racquet for a winner.

Multi-vision is stressed in all other sports. In football you see the defense constantly juggling, anticipating, trying to read the opponents by the position of their feet and shoulders or a dozen other things—they're always aware of field position and other players. Likewise, in basketball, a man on defense is always aware of his man, the ball, and his teammates and yet, at all times, he keeps his back to the goal, so he's also aware of his court position. In fact, multi-vision is taught in most sports, but in tennis the fallacy persists that if you zero in on the ball your problems are over.

The most important thing to understand, in order to progress in tennis, is triple vision. Triple vision *is* more difficult to learn than only watching the ball, but if you want a future in tennis then you must develop an awareness of all three of the dimensions of tennis. In other words, if you want to get better, if you've been stuck on a plateau for a year, two years, or ten years, the quickest way off that plateau is through the understanding of triple vision. Because if you understand the three foundations of the game, every bit of tennis knowledge and strategy and technique follows from there.

2. EYE-HAND COORDINATION

How many times have you heard a club-level player say, "Geez, I blew that last shot because I wasn't watching the ball!" But the reason he missed the shot had nothing to do with whether he watched the ball or not. I have never once had a student swing on the backhand side when the ball came to his forehand. If a ball comes to the forehand side the biggest klutz in the world will swing on the forehand side 100 percent of the time. Why? Because he already sees the ball. The reason he doesn't hit it is that he hasn't lined it up properly. In other words, he lacks the proper eye-hand coordination, and *that* is what he must develop.

There are pros who tell the student, "Watch the ball hit the strings!" Well, that's impossible. Opthalmologists tell us we begin to lose sight of the ball approximately six feet before contact. So how do you hit the ball? You line it up—just as someone who catches a ball or Frisbee behind his back (see Fig. 1) cannot see it all the way to his hand but must, instead, line it up.

Eye-hand coordination and triple vision work together. A juggler must not only have good eye-hand coordination, but also must be able to keep his attention on two or more balls at once (see Fig. 2). You can get an idea of what's involved by doing the exercise shown in Figs. 3a-c.

I was doing clinics for servicemen once in Okinawa and made the statement that in an hour I could teach anyone to hit a tennis ball back and forth across the net twenty-five times consecutively. This guy came up to me afterward and challenged me.

"My wife is so uncoordinated we have the only dishwasher in Okinawa, because she broke most of our plates washing them by hand, and we live in a one-story house because she can't walk up a flight of stairs without tripping. She's not a spastic, she's just got no coordination."

And, believe me, she was *very* uncoordinated. She's the only person to this day who I've tossed balls to who failed to hit even the frame. And I've developed the kind of toss that if you don't move your racquet the ball will hit it. If I tossed low, she'd swing high. If I tossed high, she'd swing low.

So we spent two days on eye-hand coordination drills. We tried to zero in on simple aspects—just bouncing the ball off her racquet where she couldn't miss, all the way through to the tougher drills where she'd hit it off the edge of her racquet.

Two nights later, in front of 1,000 people, including her husband, she and I hit balls. At fifteen or twenty in a row her husband began to lose his mind. He actually stood up when we got to forty or fifty, and as we kept going he started clapping like a total crazy man. This is quite a famous story now, because she and I ended up hitting 142 balls in a row over the net!

This is an important point. People assume they're uncoordinated and *that's it!* They figure they just can't learn. But, believe me, eye-hand coordination can be taught and developed. I have never failed to teach eye-hand coordination to anyone, although it is different for each person.

First of all, test your own or your children's eye-hand coordination. The following drills will help a player to develop eye-hand coordination.

Fig. 1. It's impossible to watch the ball all the way to the strings. Instead, learn to line the ball up. A Frisbee player can catch a Frisbee behind his back because he lines up the path the Frisbee will take.

Fig. 2. A simple three-ball juggling exercise can help develop dual and triple vision—being aware of more than just one object.

a.

b.

Fig. 3a. A beginning exercise in dual vision: tosser throws two balls from one hand and student catches one in each hand.

Fig. 3b. A tougher exercise in dual vision: the catcher crosses hands and catches both balls simultaneously.

Fig. 3c. Now the student tries to catch one ball and hit the other. This exercise can immediately indicate those who have natural eye-hand coordination and those who must develop it.

c.

Fig. 4a. If you're a beginner, a simple drill to help you get the feel of the racquet head is to bounce the ball up and down on the strings—known as a "self-volley." Try forehand, then backhand, then alternate forehand and backhand.

Fig. 4b. The more adept player working on eye-hand coordination drills can practice bouncing the ball in the air using only the edge of the racquet.

Self-volley drills

1. Begin simply by bouncing the ball in the air on the racquet strings with a forehand grip (see Fig. 4a). This is called a self-volley.
2. Then self-volley, alternating with hitting the ball on the racquet's edge (see Fig. 4b). Then walk doing this drill. Then jog.
3. Next self-volley on the backhand, then on edge, alternating. Then walk. Then jog.
4. Then hit a forehand self-volley with backspin. Then walk. Then jog. Then try it on the backhand side.

Fig. 5a. An excellent technique to learn racquet control is to "dribble" the ball, both with palm up (as Bernard demonstrates) and palm down (as Karen demonstrates).

Dribbling drills

1. Dribble the ball at waist height (see Fig. 5a). Then walk while dribbling. Then jog.
2. Dribble below knee height (see Fig. 5b). Then walk. Then jog.
3. Bounce the ball off the ground using the edge of the racquet (see Fig. 5c).
4. Dribble on the backhand side while using a forehand grip. Then walk. Then jog.

Fig. 5b. The next stage is to dribble below knee height, trying once again both palm up and palm down.

Fig. 5c. The third stage is to dribble the ball using only the edge of the racquet. If this is too easy, try this drill while walking or running.

Fig. 6a. The self-volley can be an exercise for lining up the ball and learning to present the racquet face to the ball.

Lining-up drills

1. Start with the simple self-volley (see Fig. 6a.).
2. Try the same thing with one racquet between your legs (see Fig. 6b).
3. Now try it with the racquet behind your back (see Fig. 6c).

Catching drills

Place the ball on the racquet strings and toss the ball into the air. Then catch the ball without letting it bounce on the strings, by reaching up toward the

b.

falling ball and cradling it on the racquet as it descends. This is called a "cradle catch." Do it on the forehand side, then the backhand side.

Playing catch with a Frisbee is also a great way to develop eye-hand coordination. Try catching the Frisbee on the run, or behind your back, or whatever trick comes to mind. All these will further develop your eye-hand coordination.

c.

Fig. 6b. This through-the-legs self-volley is not a trick shot but something that can be practiced while waiting for a court or in your backyard or driveway.

Fig. 6c. You can use your imagination to simulate all the different placements that could occur on the court, including having to hit a ball behind your back, for a real crowd pleaser.

The Three Foundations of Tennis 19

Fig. 7. Mini-tennis Stage 1—hitting back and forth in the service boxes. Mini-tennis teaches control and racquet awareness. It's also a great way to warm up, especially if you are stiff or sore or haven't played for a while. The rules are: (1) no hitting hard; (2) no volleys—you must let the ball bounce once in your court; and (3) for advanced players, all shots are hit with backspin. First player to 10 wins.

3. MINI-TENNIS

The best way I've found to teach the three foundations of tennis, especially court awareness, is through "mini-tennis." In all the years I've taught tennis, my teaching methods have constantly changed, but the one thing that has survived is mini-tennis. The basic concept of mini-tennis is to keep the ball within the confined space of the four service boxes (see Fig. 7). The first thing, of course, that everyone wants to do is whack the ball back and forth from the baseline, because that's the way the pros do it.

But think about this. In New York City a study was conducted of average club players during an hour of tennis to determine how much time was spent picking up balls and how much time was spent actually *playing* tennis. It was found that the average players spent fifty minutes picking up balls and ten minutes playing. And in New York City where court time often runs $50 an hour that's awfully expensive for ten minutes of actually playing tennis!

The great advantage of mini-tennis is that anybody can immediately begin to hit a lot of balls over the net. I've had two guys confined to wheelchairs who have hit 154 consecutive balls over from the baseline because they started with mini-tennis. I've also had a three-year-old and a man of eighty hit a hundred balls in a row over the net in their first hour of tennis. But if you start out at the baseline you may never hit a hundred in a row over in your life.

And for all you big hitters who figure mini-tennis is "puff-puff" tennis, best suited for little kids and old men, swallow your pride, because when I first saw mini-tennis it was being played by two Australians named Laver and Roche.

The idea is to learn to control the ball by first playing down-the-line mini-tennis, then cross-court mini-tennis, and then eventually full-court mini-tennis, using the entire mini-tennis area to move your opponent around (see Figs. 8, 9, 10, 11, and 12).

Mini-tennis teaches the *idea* of tennis. The focus is not on backhand or forehand but on court awareness. You learn movement, *but it's not just movement*—it's mini-movement, which is tennis movement, to take small steps in a confined space. Tennis, contrary to how most beginners gallop around the court, is not the hundred-yard dash. Also, in mini-tennis you're learning to control the ball, which in tennis means to deal with the obstruction of the net and to play in a confined area.

And, perhaps most important for the beginner, there is no overload on the mind in mini-tennis. A big complaint of all beginners trying to learn to hit the ball is, "I've got so much to remember!" There's a great mental overload in trying to learn strokes—turn sideways, change grips, step forward, racquet head down, up, sideways—"Help!" The player ends up doing everything but hitting the ball. Trying to remember more than one or two things at a time causes confusion, frustration, and lack of concentration. So move off the baselines, the freeways of tennis, and come up to the side streets and play a little mini-tennis. Remember, before you become a good tennis player (before your muscles memorize the new movements involved in tennis), you'll have to hit quite a few balls. And if you spend fifty minutes every hour picking up balls, it may take forever.

Fig. 8. As you become more adept with racquet and ball control, play mini-tennis with two or more balls in play at once.

Fig. 9. Mini-tennis Stage 2—hitting back and forth crosscourt. This helps you get the feel of direction and understand how to hit the ball where you want. Working in close gives you the opportunity to "experience" a crosscourt shot.

Fig. 10. Mini-tennis Stage 3—working in the alleys. This 4½-foot channel helps you gain control of the ball. I once saw John Newcombe and Rod Laver play an entire set using only the alleys. It's a great way to learn concentration and control.

Fig. 11. Mini-tennis Stage 4—controlling depth of shots. Set up three balls across the alleyway at the service line. Try to hit the balls. "Depth" doesn't just mean hitting deep. A good tennis player must learn to hit a variety of depths.

Fig. 12. In mini-tennis doubles, players alternate shots. Same rules as mini-tennis singles.

4. COURT AWARENESS—THE FIRST FOUNDATION

Understanding the possibilities of the court—in other words, court awareness—is a most essential step in becoming a good player. Common sense will tell you that if you don't understand the court you won't understand tennis.

Court awareness does not come naturally even to an athlete. Very few times have I seen a beginner come out and have court awareness immediately. A beginner sees only a bunch of lines, but gradually he learns there is a forecourt and backcourt, a deuce and advantage service box. But there is much more to the court than meets the untutored eye.

The Seven Target Zones

There are actually seven target zones on the court (see Diagram 1): the two deep corners, the two dropshot or dropvolley corners (those corners closest to the net), and the three "T's"—the two side T's where the service line meets the sidelines, and the center T where the center service line meets the service line.

After you learn these seven target zones you must learn to hit the ball to those spots, and the best way to develop that ability is through drills.

An excellent drill to develop your court awareness is to throw the ball to the target zones in your practice partner's court. Your partner must catch the ball on one bounce or in the air. He then throws the next "shot" and the points are played out in this manner. This drill develops your awareness of the possibilities on the court. It's also great for conditioning.

Then have one player play with a racquet and one without, and finally, have both players use racquets.

Next, you must call out *before* you hit the ball the number of the target zone you're hitting to. For advanced players, have a coach or friend call out the number of the target zone just before you hit so you have to "hold" your shot until the last second. This is also great for disguise as well as court awareness.

Positioning

Court awareness is understanding things such as angles and target zones. It is also understanding that the court position of both you and your opponent determines those angles and those possible target zones. The singles court is only twenty-seven feet wide, so most people can get to the ball as long as they know the simple strategical approach to standing in the proper position.

Basically, there are two laws covering 95 percent of all positioning problems. When the ball is in your opponent's court:

1. Shift slightly to the opposite side of the court as the ball when you're at the baseline, and to the same side when you're at the net (see Diagram 2).
2. Get back either to the Ideal Volley Position (IVP), halfway between the service line and the net, or to the baseline after each shot. (This law is only broken on a first volley, when serving and volleying—and if you're forced back on an overhead and can't regain the IVP. First volleys are usually taken around the service line, known as the Defensive Volley Position, or DVP.)

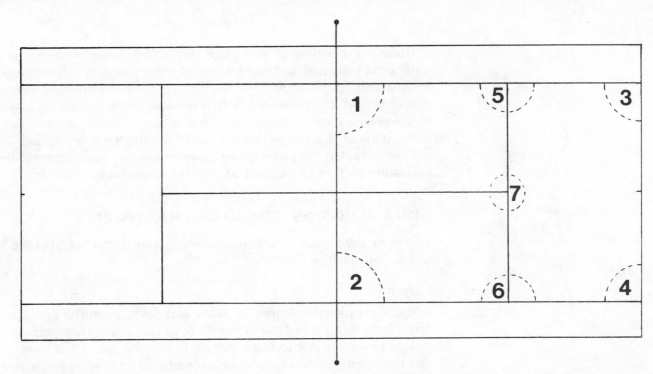

Diagram 1. There are seven basic target zones on a tennis court. 1 and 2 are the dropshot and drop-volley areas. 3 and 4 are the deep zones for penetration and eliciting a short return. 5 and 6 are the side T's (put away areas on the volley and setups for ground strokes). 7 is the center T used when an opponent can hit effective angle shots. Hitting to the center takes away his angles.

Diagram 2. The dotted lines bisect at the "actual" center of the court (not the center T, as most people believe). By drawing a line from the ball through this "actual" center of the court, you can calculate your proper court position for any shot. As you can see, you should only get back to the "middle" (at the center stripe) for balls hit down the "middle" of your opponent's court. Otherwise, as rule 2 of court positioning states, if you are at the baseline, shift slightly to the opposite side of the court from the ball; if you are at the net, shift to the same side as the ball.

COURT POSITIONING FOR SINGLES

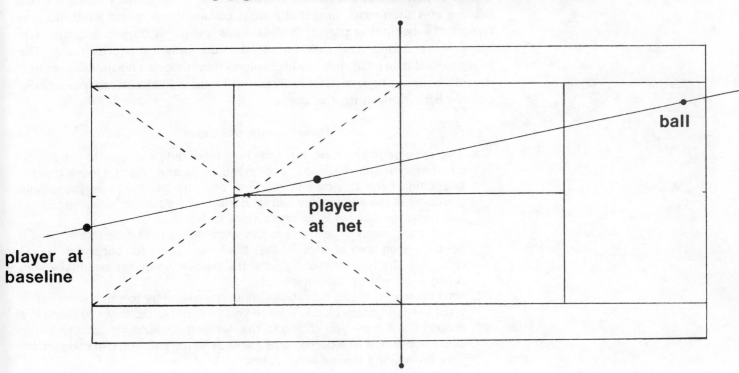

These two positioning laws place you in the center of where the greatest number of balls will likely be hit, and therefore they are the ideal positions from which to get most balls. Of course, if your opponent can only hit crosscourt, which is common with beginning and intermediate players, then by all means cheat crosscourt from where you know the ball is coming.

If you follow these rules you will rarely be caught out of position—and that will immediately improve your game, because most intermediate and beginning players are almost *always* out of position.

5. BALL AWARENESS—THE SECOND FOUNDATION

There are three areas of ball awareness: (1) spin, (2) the height of the ball, and (3) the ball itself.

Spin

Many people play tennis for years and never learn the first thing about spin—how to hit it or how to handle it. In fact, when I first started teaching tennis, I was told not to teach people how to hit spin for at least two years. But there are several important reasons to hit with spin. Perhaps the most important, is that only two things make the ball land in the court—gravity and spin. Beginners use gravity to vary depth in their opponent's court by hitting harder or softer, and more advanced players use spin. The pros can hit the ball very hard and make it stay in because they use spin. But spin, contrary to what most club players believe, is not just for power. It should be used principally to gain control over the ball.

You can vary both the depth and the height of the ball through spin. But more important you should use more spin in emergencies, particularly backspin, because the ball travels more slowly and gives you more time to recover. Also, backspin is your control spin (topspin is your power spin), and you must try for maximum control in emergencies.

How to handle a spinning ball is another matter. Beginners watch the ball bounce and then react, and that's what causes those quick, jerky motions typical of a beginning player. Professionals are rarely fooled, because they learn to recognize the different spins and how each will react. The fundamental rule in understanding spin is that backspin bounces lower and topspin bounces higher. Also, backspin will tend to float and topspin will dip quickly back down into the court.

Drills to understand spin

1. If you're a beginner, have someone hit a lot of different spins to you so you can observe what happens. Just stand there and watch. Heavy topspin bouncing at the service line will land *past* the baseline; heavy backspin bouncing at the service line will land *inside* the baseline; sidespin will act like backspin but tends to curve right or left.

   The conclusion of this drill is to watch the racquet face to see what it does on each type of shot. At first it will take you a full second or two to recognize the type of spin by what the racquet does, but eventually your recognition will be instantaneous.
2. Now have your friend hit various spins at you and try to catch each ball at waist level. A topspin lob will force you to sprint to the fence to catch it, a dropshot will have you racing to the net. But because you don't have to worry about how or where *you're* going to hit the ball, you can concentrate fully on reading the different spins.

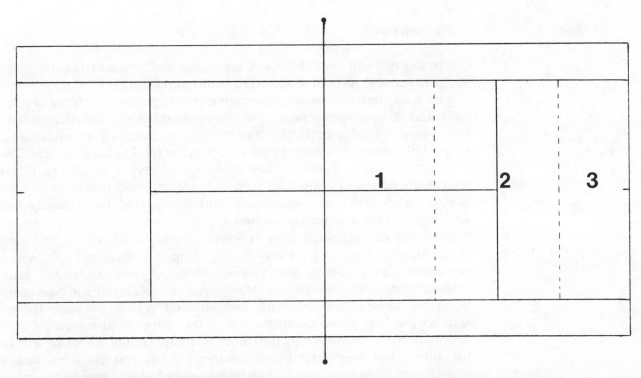

Diagram 3. Anticipation drill. The height at which the ball clears the net relates to how deep the ball will land in the court. As a practice drill, call out the area (1, 2, or 3) where you think your opponent's ball will land by using the height of the ball to gauge how deep the ball will land in your court. Try calling out as soon as the ball leaves your opponent's racquet. This will greatly aid your anticipation.

Height of the Ball

Generally, on a medium-paced ball, the height at which the ball clears the net relates to how deep it lands on the court. Most people, however, have no idea what's going to happen when the ball goes high or low over the net. Generally, a ball that clears the net by a lot will land deep and a ball that barely clears the net will land short. Obviously, this varies according to the speed and trajectory.

A good player can determine what the height of the ball will be as soon as his opponent hits it, or at the very latest as it crosses the net. That's why, many times, on a let-cord shot a pro will often get to the ball quite easily, whereas a club player watches it fall for a winner and mumbles to himself how lucky his opponent is. The reason the pro gets to the ball has nothing to do with luck, and it's not that he's that much faster than the average club player, but just that he's *anticipating* better.

Here's a drill that will improve your ball awareness almost immediately. Divide your side of the court up into three areas, as shown in Diagram 3:

1. Up close to the net
2. In the middle
3. Very deep

As soon as the ball leaves the opponent's racquet, call out "One," "Two," or "Three" according to the area in which you think the ball will land. In the beginning you'll often be wrong, but after ten or fifteen minutes you'll begin to pinpoint where the ball will land. Imagine what this will do for your game.

The Ball Itself

A tennis ball will react differently according to the type of ball, the type of surface, and the elements, including wind and altitude.

A rose may be a rose by any other name, but there are many types of tennis balls, and no two types act the same. There are dozens of different brands of balls—Penn, Slazenger, Tretorn, and Dunlop, to name a few—and they all play a little differently. Some bounce high, some tend to float, some are fast, and some are slow. There are also many specific types of balls: hard-core, heavy-duty nap, and nonpressurized balls usually tend to play slower and heavier, while soft-core, regular-nap, and pressurized balls usually have added pace and a tendency to float.

Hit a few of the match balls in warm-up and try to adjust your game accordingly. For example, a very heavy, nonpressurized ball will tend to neutralize power serves and prolong rallies. A serve-and-volley game, therefore, becomes less effective. Many professionals study the type of ball being played very carefully. Marty Riessen used to wear the same colored shirt as the ball, so he could get that extra split-second advantage if his opponent had trouble picking the ball up as it came out of the background of his shirt. That may sound a bit extreme until you consider that in tournament table tennis *only* dark, solid-colored shirts may be worn.

The court surface is a significant factor in the way the ball will react. A clay court will "grab" the ball and make it bounce up more slowly than a grass or hard court will. This means on clay you can track down a lot more balls that would be outright winners on other surfaces. On grass the ball takes erratic bounces. You never really know what it will do, except that backspin shots stay extremely low, sometimes never coming up at all. Conversely, hard courts usually yield a steady, "true" bounce. The important thing is to get out before a match and experience the court surface and note how the ball reacts to the court.

Finally, you should be aware of what wind and altitude can do to a tennis ball. Be aware of the direction and speed of the wind on your face and legs and learn what a ball will do—whether it will curve left or right, bounce low or high. Also, a fair percentage of the world's population lives at a significant altitude. In rarefied air the ball will float and travel much faster; therefore, the chances of its staying in are much less. That's why "high-altitude" balls are used in places like Colorado, Mexico City, and Bolivia.

6. OPPONENT AWARENESS—THE THIRD FOUNDATION

Anticipation

We'd all be Wimbledon champs if no one was on the other side of the net. But you must learn to deal with an opponent and to counter that opponent's strategy.

Most players stop concentrating once the ball is off their racquet. They're thinking, "Did I look good?" or "Did I feel good?" rather than zeroing in on what's going on in the opponent's court. Once that ball leaves your racquet you should be thinking solely about what the ball is doing in your opponent's court and where and what your opponent's next shot will be.

This is known as *anticipation*, and it has always been considered a very advanced bit of tennis knowledge. But I teach anticipation to beginners almost immediately.

Primarily, anticipation is the ability to have a reasonably good idea where your opponent's shot is going before he hits it. But anticipation is also determining what the ball will do in terms of spin and height, getting off the mark on time, and positioning yourself according to what you know will happen.

Reading Your Opponent's Racquet

Ultimately, the ball is going to do what the racquet makes it do, so if you understand what happens to the ball when the opponent's racquet face does certain things then you'll be developing anticipation.

First you should be aware of how your opponent is setting up his racquet—whether he's taking a big backswing, medium backswing, or no backswing (see Fig. 13), and whether the face is open or closed (see Figs. 14 and 15a-b). For example, if his racquet face is open just prior to contact it will

Fig. 13. If your opponent takes a huge backswing, it usually indicates that he intends to hit hard.

Fig. 14. *If your opponent opens his racquet face prior to contacting the ball, it usually means a backspin shot is coming.*

probably be a backspin shot and you'll know the ball is going to bounce low, travel a little more slowly, and, perhaps, float. Secondly, be aware of what his racquet does after contacting the ball—if his racquet finishes high and on edge, chances are it will be a topspin (see Fig. 16a); if his racquet finishes at the same level at which he contacted the ball or lower and the strings point to the sky, it's sure to be a backspin shot (see Fig. 16b).

Anticipation and Your Opponent's Position

Anticipation is linked to the word "limitation." Your opponent may be limited to one or two possible shots by his position on the court. In other words, the better shot you hit, the more limited your opponent is. If you hit a great shot his only return will probably be a lob. A deep approach to his backhand will severely limit your opponent's shot selection, and if you know he has trouble going crosscourt you've limited him further. Or, if your opponent is three feet from the net and the ball is bouncing low you know quite a number of things. For example, he can't hit hard, and in order to clear the net he must put an arc on the ball, which means the ball will probably sit up nicely for you.

Fig. 15a. A closed racquet face will usually mean topspin. Peter shows a closed racquet face on the forehand side here.

Fig. 15b. A closed racquet face on the backhand side.

Fig. 16a. A player hitting a topspin ground stroke will usually finish with the racquet above the head and on edge.

Fig. 16b. On a backspin ground stroke, the racquet face finishes "open" to the sky or relatively parallel to the ground.

Disguise

Disguise and anticipation are inseparable because reading disguise *is* anticipation. In order to understand your opponent's racquet you must understand your own. Basically, disguise is being able to do everything the same on every shot right up until the moment of contact. If you make the same racquet preparation on every shot (see Figs. 17a and 17b), then you'll be learning disguise. And as you progress as a player, this becomes more and more significant.

Fig. 17a. On a well-disguised shot, the feet, shoulders, and racquet tell very little about what is to come. All variations of shots are comfortably possible and practical from this preparation.

Fig. 17b. If your foot and racquet preparation is the same on every backhand, you'll disguise which direction you intend to hit the ball.

Fig. 18a. You can often detect the direction a player is going to hit the ball by watching the way he positions his feet. Almost every player I've ever played, from beginner to circuit player, "tipped off" his shot this way. An open stance on the backhand indicates a player is going to hit cross-court because it's very difficult to hit down-the-line backhands from an open stance.

Fig. 18b. An excessive crossover step usually means a down-the-line shot is coming.

Fig. 19a. Many players will give away the direction of their ground strokes through the positioning of their shoulders. Premature opening of the shoulders usually means the player will hit crosscourt.

b.

Fig. 19b. An excessive shoulder turn often means that the ball will be hit down the line.

Disguise, like anticipation, has also been considered a very advanced technique. But I teach disguise in the first year, because the whole concept of my teaching is to instruct the beginner the same as the advanced player. However, I teach the beginner simple disguise—not so much to disguise his own shots as to read disguise, so he'll know, for example, that when his opponent's racquet head drops down low it's probably going to be a lob. Some of the giveaways are shown in Figs. 18 a-b, 19 a-b, 20 and 21.

Fig. 20. If your opponent lifts his lead heel (the heel closest to the net) while hitting a ground stroke, it usually means he lacks confidence in that shot.

Fig. 21. A beginning or intermediate player will often give away the lob by dropping his racquet lower than on a regular ground stroke.

Fig. 22a. On the serve, watch your opponent's toss. Usually a player will give away his serve by his toss. Many players will toss the ball farther to the right when serving a slice serve.

Fig. 22b. For a topspin serve, the same player will toss the ball over his head and to the left.

Fig. 22c. For a flat serve, most players will toss straight ahead—which is actually the toss that you should use for all serves because it offers greater potential for disguise.

The game has become so sophisticated that players now strive for more and more disguise. For instance, the old way of teaching the serve was to toss the ball to the right for a spin serve, straight ahead for flat, and back over the head for topspin. This is not advisable because you're tipping off your serve (see Figs. 22a-c and 23a-b).

a.

b.

In this chapter I've tried to give you an understanding of the game of tennis by introducing some important fundamentals. But I hope after you've read this book you won't go around telling everyone, "Oh, well, Burwash said to do it this way." *Your own understanding is more important than what I say.* My goal is not to teach you Burwash's way to play tennis, but to teach you how to play your own game. I'm not teaching a system, I'm teaching individuals. Not form, but understanding.

Also, I stress continuity. That is, the beginner is taught the same fundamentals as the advanced player, because common sense will tell you a fundamental will work for all levels of play or it's not a fundamental. It's important to know that some totally bad teaching will sometimes help a student hit the ball over the net at that moment. But what feels good immediately and what's right for way down the road are often two different things. A good game is built on a solid foundation of fundamentals. The advanced player builds his game on the same basics as the beginner, but he learns more details, more drills, and more variations so that he is constantly refining his game.

Fig. 23a. Sometimes you can determine the direction that your opponent intends to serve by watching the placement of his back foot. The back foot positioned to the left often indicates a wide serve (to the deuce court).

Fig. 23b. When the back foot (right) appears behind the lead foot, this indicates a probable down-the-center serve (to the deuce court). If a player hits all his serves from one position, then, of course, this does not apply. Many players, however, do use different foot positions to serve in different directions.

Phase Two
How to Be Your Own Coach
Part I:
Understanding Strokes

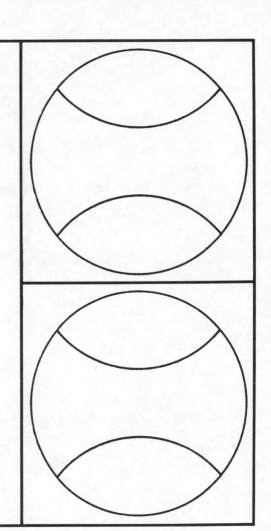

Chapter Four
Why Be Your Own Coach?

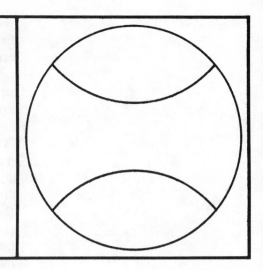

One year at Wimbledon, after I'd been bombed out in a very early round, I sat with Rod Laver in the grandstands and we got to talking as we watched a match. I asked him, "Who do you go to when you're in trouble?" His reply in that typical, matter-of-fact Aussie tone was, "I go to myself."

Whether you want to or not, you must eventually learn to coach yourself. When you're in the middle of a match and you're hitting too long or too short, what do you do? Or your opponent suddenly starts rushing the net, volleying like a madman, and you find you can't hit a passing shot that day. Or you can't hit deep or your serve has crumbled. Who do you go to for advice right there in the middle of a match? Your opponent? No, you've got to go to yourself. Your goal should be to become a self-sufficient tennis player so you can win even when your strokes desert you.

As I've said before, I stress common-sense tennis—in other words, doing what's practical. The dictionary defines "practical" as "anything that stresses opposition to all that is theoretical, speculative, ideal, or unrealistic and implies a relation to the actual life of man, his problems and needs."

There's been too much talk, too much theorizing, too many so-called "scientific studies" done in recent years on how to hit a tennis ball. All this endless research is the result of a bad direction in tennis—the overintellectualizing of a stroke. There are no miracles that research will dig up. A great topspin backhand takes years of hard work and talent, and it doesn't come just by reading or hitting endlessly off a ball machine. It comes from playing under pressure and adjusting under pressure.

How will it benefit you to know, for example, that the racquet recoils on contact? That fact is insignificant unless you're on some grand level of the game, and it's very unlikely that you ever will be—circuit players constitute a very small segment of all the people who play tennis. Why get all befuddled with overcomplication?

There are things you must do to hit successful strokes, but the mechanics of the swing are relatively simple. If you're way out of position and you have to run a mile just to get to the ball, and then you try some shot you can't make in a dream, all the textbooks in the world are not going to help you. What you don't seem to understand is that even Borg would have lobbed *that* shot.

Hitting the ball is not such a difficult task. If you'd stop trying to do 900 things at once you'd probably hit plenty of winners. Instead, simplify—use your common sense. You must have simple adjustments so that they can be functional in a pressure situation when the mind can usually handle only one thing at a time. Most important, however, you must understand the cause and the result of what you do with your racquet in order to make the proper corrective adjustments. For example, if I ask a club-level player at the end of a match to tell me what his mistakes were, he usually can't do it. He'll say, "Oh, I guess I didn't watch the ball." Or a player will come to me and say, "I'm having trouble with my backhand," so I'll ask, "What's wrong?" and he'll usually answer, "I don't know. I just can't hit it."

Most players have certain identifiable weaknesses. They make the same specific errors over and over, but they haven't really thought about what they're doing wrong, whether the ball is going long or short or wide. The problem is that most players only look at a shot closely if it's good—they're basking in the glory of their great shot. And if they flub one they close their eyes in agony before the ball has even landed. The key, however, to correcting your own game is watching what happens to your own errors. What was the result of that horrible backhand? Did it go into the net? Did you hit it on the throat? Remember, before you can correct your mistake you have to know what went wrong.

Phases Two and Three—"How to Be Your Own Coach," Part One and Part Two—are designed to show you how to give yourself corrective lessons right in the middle of the match. So if your game falls apart you can quickly and systematically analyze your problems right on the court. In order to correct your strokes, however, you've got to build them on solid fundamentals of understanding. There are three fundamentals of sound stroking—contact area, balance, and the use of the left hand (Chapter Five)—that you can use to build your entire understanding of how to hit the ball. Then there are the five dimensions of the stroke—getting it in, direction, depth, spin, and speed (Chapter Six)—with which you can develop your understanding of what to do *with* the ball. Along with this general understanding of the stroke I will show you how to develop "simplicity checkpoints" (Chapters Seven to Twelve), which correct the particular, idiosyncratic breakdowns of your individual stroke, because everyone inevitably develops his or her own style and with it his or her own particular problems. The three fundamentals and the five dimensions of a stroke are the general understanding, and the simplicity checkpoints are the particular correction.

But let me stress again, the basis of "self-coaching" is common sense. I can't tell you what you should do in every situation. You must take the information that I supply and develop the correctional techniques and gimmicks that will work for you. In a match, you must learn to use your head, because it's the only one you've got. Then if it gets down to the crunch in the last set, like Rod Laver, you can go to yourself for help.

Chapter Five
The Three Fundamentals of Sound Stroking:
Contact Area, Balance, and the Use of the Left Hand

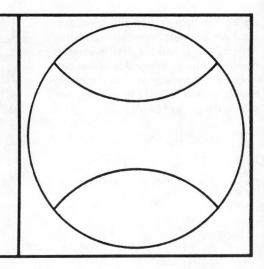

The first step in becoming your own coach is to understand the three fundamentals of sound stroking—(1) contact area; (2) balance; and (3) the use of the left hand.

1. CONTACT AREA

There are three parts to the typical stroke—the backswing, the contact area (the area where the racquet and ball are in contact), and the follow-through. By far the most important of these three is the contact area.

The entire game of tennis, quite logically, centers around the moment when the racquet strings contact the ball. Everything—backswing, follow-through, footwork, concentration, preparation, strings, shoes, you name it— is secondary to that moment. You can have the greatest-looking backswing and the greatest-looking follow-through, but if the contact area is not correct, you won't hit the ball effectively.

The best way to correct problems with the contact area is to play mini-tennis. There is no backswing or follow-through in mini-tennis, so you must concentrate on simply contacting the ball. One of the first things I do, in fact, when someone is too preoccupied with backswing and follow-through, is to take away their follow-through, and immediately they begin to hit the ball in the center of the strings. As a practice exercise, just freeze your swing at the point of contact and concentrate on pointing your strings toward the intended target. This gives you a feel for presentation of the racquet head.

The main mistake a typical player will develop in hitting the ball is overcomplicating the path that the racquet takes. As he swings he does funny things with his arm or wrist, instead of simply realizing that the racquet head is an extension of his hand. Just because you have that extra thirty inches in your hand doesn't mean you start wielding it like a sword. The path of the racquet head should be consistent with the path of the hand.

A useful method to ensure that you are pointing the racquet strings toward your target is to keep your wrist and racquet head moving together. A slapping motion is created when the racquet head flies ahead of the wrist as you swing. So if you think "wrist and racquet head together" as you point the strings, it will help to control the racquet head.

Another way of visualizing this is thinking "palm forward." The racquet

Fig. 24. The bottom three fingers of the hand are the most important to maintain a strong and a firm but flexible wrist. The thumb and index finger should just be wrapped comfortably around the racquet handle, as they do not play a significant role in the ground stroke.

head, no matter how you swing, will only go where the palm goes, so if you zero in on the palm as you swing, you will know where your racquet face is pointing. On the backhand think "knuckles forward."

Also, if your strokes are crumbling (or you never had any strokes to start with), slow down your swing. We all want to crunch that ball, but when you're not hitting well, one of the most fundamental corrective techniques is to pretend your arm is in a slow-motion movie. In this way your mind can begin to perceive what your body is up to. It's simple enough, but how many times have you seen a player, who has lost his touch, start to hit harder and harder trying to get it back? It's obviously foolish, but that mixture of panic and pride just won't let him slow down.

Another method to practice control of the racquet head is to try choking up on the racquet, because the longer the racquet, the greater the weight at the racquet head and the greater the tendency to slap at the ball. If you move your hand up the handle you'll have more control over the racquet head and a better understanding when you return to the full grip.

The technique I emphasize the most, however, in correcting problems with the contact area is to firm up the wrist. More than any single factor, a firm wrist enables a player to control the path of the racquet head. When your wrist is floppy, flying around out of control, your palm is also out of control. Your wrist is the link between your body and your racquet, and if you have a weak link you have a weak shot.

The proper technique for hitting with a firm wrist is not, as many believe, to squeeze harder with your entire hand, because your index finger and thumb have very little to do with controlling the wrist. Only the last three fingers of the hand are connected anatomically with the set of tendons that control the tightening of the wrist. So if you concentrate on squeezing those three fingers the wrist will firm up nicely (see Fig. 24).

An easy check you can make to see if you have a firm wrist is to note the presence of what is known as the "anatomical snuffbox," the indentation at the base of the thumb, on the outside of your hand. For most people it will automatically appear if the wrist is firm and in the proper position (see Fig. 25).

The only time you want a loose wrist is in an extreme emergency situation, when you want to get the ball over any way you can. A flexible wrist can be very useful at those times.

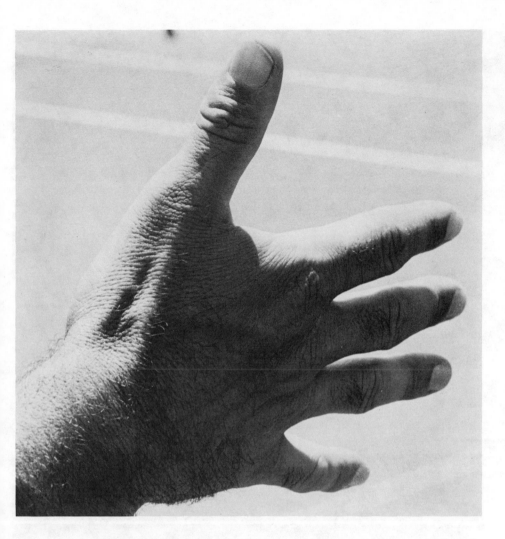

Seven Times You Don't Take Your Racquet Back

Whenever tennis is taught you'll hear the phrase "racquet back." That seems to be the most frequently used instruction for beginning tennis players—"Get your racquet back!" And that one phrase has probably destroyed more potentially good tennis players than any other piece of advice. The racquet back/follow-through brand of coaching ignores the most important part of the game—the contact area, or hitting the ball.

In fact, there are seven times when you do *not* take the racquet back:

1. On a hard-hit ball
2. On a volley
3. On a half-volley
4. On a ball hit right at you
5. When you're slow physically
6. When you're slow mentally
7. When you're slow physically and mentally

Fig. 26a. On a hard-hit ball, eliminate backswing, present the racquet face to the ball, and use your opponent's pace to your advantage.

Fig. 26b. Many players try to take a full backswing on a hard-hit ball. If you take your racquet all the way back, the ball may be past you before you know it.

Fig. 27. On volleys, eliminate the back-swing. A person who learns to play tennis by the "racquet back" method usually has trouble understanding and "feeling" the volley.

ON A HARD-HIT BALL

The first thing most players do when the ball has been blasted at them is to try to hit it back even harder. Most players just don't have time on an extremely hard-hit ball to get the racquet back. Just present the racquet face to the ball and let the natural rebound of the strings, the minimum potential, provide the pace on the ball (see Fig. 26a). The ball will go back with plenty on it, and best of all it will probably land in. But if you take a huge backswing, the ball may be past you before you swing at it (see Fig. 26b). At the very least, you'll swing late and the ball will end up three courts down.

This situation frequently occurs when you play an opponent who hits much harder than you're accustomed to. Instead of trying to hit as hard or harder than your opponent, you should simply use the stronger player's pace to your advantage.

ON A VOLLEY

In most cases it's natural to bring the racquet back on the volley, because for so long every pro kept drilling in, "Racquet back!" That's why so often a player has problems learning the volley. He is programmed to take his racquet back, so as soon as he sees the ball his immediate instinctual reaction is "racquet back." Whether the ball is in the air, on the ground, whether it's coming fast or slow—back goes his racquet. That's why I teach contact area first and introduce the backswing later.

Think of all the people who get their racquet back quickly. Even someone as phenomenally successful as Chris Evert. Yet how well does Evert volley? Still, to this day, you'll sometimes see Chris swinging on a volley. You only take the racquet back *if you have time*, and on the volley you usually don't have time.

On the volley you don't need to supply a lot of power, so you don't need a big backswing (see Fig. 27). There is a tremendous amount of rebound in the

Fig. 28. Another time you don't take your racquet back is on the half-volley. The half-volley is an emergency. Most players hit a half-volley because they're forced into it, not because they like to.

strings. Besides, in the Ideal Volley Position (halfway between the net and the service line), a player is only fifty-two feet from the baseline and a putaway volley to a side T will travel only twenty-five to thirty feet. If you're volleying at the net, then, there's no question that you'll have enough power. It's a question of control—will you be able to keep it in?

ON A HALF-VOLLEY

The half-volley is a defensive shot. No one wants to hit a half-volley. Usually a player is forced into that situation because the opponent has hit a strong shot at your feet. If the opponent hits a soft floater you can step back and take it on the full bounce or move up quickly and take it in the air. So, if played correctly, you should only be hitting half-volleys off balls that are hit

Fig. 29a. When you're at the net and the ball is hit directly at you, use your back-hand volley. This is one of the seven times you don't take your racquet back.

fairly hard, and therefore your minimum potential, the natural rebound off your strings, will be great enough so that you won't need much power to hit the ball deep (see Fig. 28).

ON A BALL HIT RIGHT AT YOU

It's difficult for many players to accept that if the ball is hit directly at you, you're in a defensive position and should simply try to block the ball back with a minimum amount of backswing (see Fig. 29a). When a ball is hit right at you you're extremely vulnerable. That's why in doubles, for instance, it's smart to aim for the opponent's right hip, because that's where he's most vulnerable (see Fig. 29b).

Fig. 29b. For a ball hit at your right hip, it is virtually impossible to take the volley on the forehand side. Many beginners will try some awkward acrobatics until someone instructs them how to do it properly.

WHEN YOU'RE SLOW PHYSICALLY OR MENTALLY OR BOTH PHYSICALLY AND MENTALLY

These apply to beginners as well as guys playing at the French Open in Paris, who are in the fifth set of one of those clay-court marathons and are physically fatigued and lose all concentration. Those pros will begin to hit the ball with an extremely abbreviated backswing because their legs have had it and their arms weigh a ton and they'll do anything they can to just get it back. So they zero in on contact and live off their opponent's pace.

Beginners are usually slow physically because they're not reacting properly to the ball coming at them. And they're slow mentally because they're confused by the new situation—they have so much to remember. So, the best advice for a beginner or someone who is fatigued or just doesn't move well on the court is simply to concentrate on contact area. It's not necessary to take a big backswing.

Racquet Preparation

Instead of "racquet back," I use the term "racquet preparation," with the implied understanding that there are many times when you hit a ball without taking your racquet back. Basically, you should prepare your racquet according to the speed of the ball. The slower the ball, the farther you can take your racquet back, because the purpose of the backswing is to add power, to hit the ball harder. And if the ball is already coming hard there's no need to add more pace to it. That's the essence of "racquet preparation" as opposed to "racquet back." In other words, you should take your racquet back *when you have time*—which may be on every shot if you're playing a weak player.

When I play a strong player I can usually take the racquet only about three-quarters back at most. Now imagine most beginning or intermediate players who have all those things to remember. Sure you can take a big swat when someone is tossing balls to you or when you're playing the club pushover. But anyone who understands tennis is not likely to feed you those setups in a match.

Your racquet preparation is also determined by the circumstances. For example, if the court surface is very fast concrete you should shorten your backswing, whereas on clay you usually have time for a picnic before you swing. Consequently, you see a lot of clay-court players with long looping backswings. Also, if there's a heavy wind playing tricks with the ball, or if you're playing under lights and the visibility is poor, or if the balls are new and therefore very quick, then again you should shorten your backswing.

Finally, if you're playing an opponent who always takes his racquet back immediately on every shot, try "slow-balling" him. His muscles are so tense from holding the racquet back for so long that the trigger often goes off just ahead of time and he'll end up hitting crosscourt on every shot. It is a very fine triggering of the neurons we're dealing with here, and it really doesn't take all that much to throw off a solid hit. So if you change up speeds frequently on a "racquet back" player you'll often force him into mishits.

The Follow-through

The final element of a typical stroke is the follow-through, and, contrary to popular belief, it has nothing to do with hitting a good shot, because by definition the follow-through begins the moment the ball leaves the racquet strings. The only purposes of the follow-through are to prevent injury and to complete a natural motion.

It's very dangerous to stop your swing immediately after hitting the ball. If you stop your swing abruptly the result can often be a muscle pull or tendon strain—in other words, common ailments such as tennis elbow.

The correct follow-through is a simple common-sense thing. Usually, problems only begin when you do *too much* with the follow-through—wrapping it around your neck or rolling the wrist over at the end to try to put all sorts of fancy spin on the ball. Basically, just let your arm flow through freely and the follow-through will occur naturally.

2. BALANCE

The most difficult task in tennis is getting from one place to another. If you can get to the ball I can teach you to hit it. Hitting the ball, as I've said before, is not all that difficult. But getting to the ball so you're ready to hit a good shot *is* difficult.

Just because you're fast does not mean you can get to the ball effectively, because the beginning and the end of the run are the most important parts of getting to the ball. First of all, the player who gets a quick start has anticipated what his opponent will do (see Phase One, "Understanding the Game"), and in most cases could probably get to the ball on crutches. And secondly, once you get to the ball, speed is meaningless. The important question becomes—are you balanced?

Balance Versus Footwork

Forget footwork. All this elaborate teaching of footwork does nothing but confuse. It puts too much of a mental overload on you. You can move around a lot, turn sideways, move your shoulders and feet in a certain way, and yet you may fail to accomplish your original goal—to hit the ball over the net.

I knew a pro who actually painted steps on the court to show you where each foot should go as you set up for a shot. Now, that's ridiculous! Who really has the time in a match to calculate exactly where to put each foot? Besides, no two shots are ever hit the same.

Footwork is secondary to balance. In fact, footwork is just a technique for maintaining balance while hitting a shot. The concentration of a player who learns footwork, therefore, is all wrong. The mental focus is directed to the feet when it should be directed to the bellybutton, which is the center of gravity—at least, in males. (The center of gravity in women is slightly lower, which gives them better balance. The higher center of gravity in males gives them greater speed.) So it's not footwork you want to learn at all, but balance.

A body is in balance when the center of gravity—the bellybutton—is over the top of the base, which, of course, is the feet. To determine the size of your base, simply take a piece of chalk and draw a rectangle on the ground around the heels and toes of both feet, so that you've drawn the little area that you stand in.

It's natural to be in balance. That's why players will do such strange things with their feet on a tennis court in order to maintain balance. They look uncoordinated and hopelessly inept, but, actually, they're doing what nature intended—staying in balance. You'll see players spin around, go up in the air, lean backward, anything they can do not to fall over. These are all natural compensations the body makes to stay in balance. So people are, by nature, balanced. Only very infrequently do players fall on the court, for example, because they know instinctively, long before they fall, that they're off-balance, and that great computer, the mind, instantaneously cries for help and the body makes the proper adjustments.

How do you prevent yourself, then, from going through all those unnecessary motions in order to maintain your balance? First of all, your feet must be a reasonable distance apart so you create a base of balance. Then be sure your bellybutton does not lean outside that base. Once it does you're off-balance.

Fig. 30. *A checkpoint in practice to establish good balance and a wide base is to place a racquet lengthwise between your feet after contact. Or, if you're practicing with a ball machine, you can put a racquet down prior to contact.*

Fig. 31. *On low balls, your center of gravity should be lowered. A simple guideline to checkpoint yourself in practice is an approximate 90-degree bend in both legs.*

The best technique for creating better balance is simply to bend your knees. Our base is a very narrow rectangle much longer than it is wide and, therefore, very unstable. It's very easy to lose your balance. But by dropping your bellybutton down (by bending your knees) you lower your center of gravity, thereby creating a more stable base. It's like one of those inflatable dolls with the sand in the feet—it's almost impossible to knock it off-balance. That's why a player who is aware of the balance factor will drop his center of gravity if he's losing his balance.

A beginner often makes the mistake, however, of bending at the waist, thus throwing his weight outside the base of the feet. So he's out of balance before he begins to move. Is it any wonder that he has trouble getting to the ball?

Drills to stress balance

1. A gimmick to learn better balance is to concentrate on just one part of your body. For instance, put all the weight on your lead foot and bend your lead knee at a 90-degree angle as you hit (or you can also lower your back knee). This focuses your mind on the task of maintaining the proper balance throughout a point because you're concentrating on your body balance (see Fig. 30).
2. Have a friend hit and you play without a racquet, catching the balls. This eliminates any distractions created by the racquet or setting up to hit the ball. You can concentrate on getting to the ball in balance.
3. Freeze after you hit each shot and see if you can place your racquet flat on the ground between your feet while maintaining your balance. This is a handy check to see if you have the proper base for good balance (see Fig. 31).
4. Try hitting everything with two hands—both the forehand and backhand. This forces you to set up closer to the ball. This is a more balanced position.
5. Study yourself in a balanced position—feet spread apart, knees bent, head and bellybutton over the top of the base—and create a visual picture of it. Practice it in front of a mirror until you know what it "feels" like without looking.

Body Weight and Power

Another myth about footwork is that you should "step into the ball," thereby transferring your weight into the ball for greater power. But the transference of body weight on ground strokes has nothing to do with power. PBI did a test in Los Angeles with the radar speed gun comparing the speed that a player could hit a forehand with both a "closed" (with the shoulder sideways to the net) and "open" (or facing the net) stance. We found virtually no difference. In fact, many could hit slightly *harder* with an open stance (see Figs. 32a-b).

Now what's significant about this test is that on an open-stance forehand your weight transfer is actually going toward the sideline—not toward the net. It's physically impossible to get your weight going toward the net, because from the hips down you're stationary. Therefore, it's your arm that supplies most of the power. Even on a closed-stance forehand your weight transfer (from the back to the front foot) should occur before the ball is contacted, not *during* the stroke (see Fig. 33).

Fig. 32a. The open-stance forehand is hit with the weight on the right foot. PBI tests with radar speed guns showed that the speed of a player's forehand varied little whether it was hit from an open or closed stance.

Fig. 32b. The open-stance forehand is very valuable on wide shots.

Fig. 33. *On ground strokes the weight transfer should occur* before *you contact the ball, not* during *the shot.*

There are pros who teach that weight transfer should occur simultaneously with the contact of the ball and the swing of the arm. Their students have incredible problems with timing, especially in special circumstances, such as bad bounces or wind or when playing a junk-baller or a spin artist. If you try to time your weight transfer to coincide with the exact moment you contact the ball and the ball goes off course even the slightest bit, you'll be incapable of making the necessary adjustments. It's far more difficult to suddenly change the direction of your entire body than to make a simple arm or wrist adjustment.

What creates pace is timing, and timing is being able to connect with the ball in the center of the racquet at exactly the right instant for maximum power and control. A so-called "heavy" ball is created by timing, not weight transfer, as evidenced by someone like Arthur Ashe, who has very small biceps but can hit one of the fastest serves in the world because of his superb timing.

The classic example of this occurred in Los Angeles, where PBI held a fast-serving contest. We had several players from the National Football League and we had two 85-pound twelve-year olds, and the kids could serve faster than the 250-pound football players. The football players could pick the kids up with one hand, yet their serves were, on the average, 10 mph slower.

Hitting Off-balance

There are many times in a match when you will not be able to hit on balance. Your opponent has you climbing the fences, chasing balls or twisting and turning, trying to hit overheads. So what do you do?

The key to hitting an effective shot when off-balance or on the run is the "disassociation" of the upper part of your body from the lower. The biggest mistake you can make while chasing a ball at full speed is to let the momentum of your feet transfer to your racquet head and overpower the ball. Instead of racing fifty feet to get to the ball and then hitting it fifty feet out, your idea should be to disassociate your arms from your feet. Run as hard as you can to get to the ball, but never let your arm maintain that speed at point of contact. You should have "fast feet" and a "slow arm."

If you're off-balance, you're in an extremely weak position. You're on defense and your objective should be to neutralize the opponent. Most players, however, try to do too much with the ball. For some reason they think they should hit their best passing shots when they're off-balance. On off-balance shots, however, contact area is critical, because when you're off-balance you're in an emergency situation. And in emergency situations you should always limit the motion of the racquet face. In other words, simply present the racquet face to the ball. Don't get fancy; don't try a shot you haven't made in ten years.

Hitting on the Run

Hitting on the run presents its own problems. There are many times on a running shot, for instance, when you don't take your racquet back at all because you can run faster by pumping both arms. Players conditioned to run with their racquets back can't move as well because there's a natural drag on the body when running with the racquet back.

If you're running laterally, the tendency is to hit a short ball. You'll tend to compensate for your lateral movement by swinging your arm back toward where you came from, so that on a forehand your racquet will end up over your left shoulder. This creates a very short contact area and therefore a very short ball.

Don't let the lateral direction of your feet influence the direction in which your palm moves. The correction is to exaggerate the "palm forward" movement in order to lengthen your contact and hit deep.

Recovery Steps

Of course, if you're a smart player you'll try to stay balanced so that you're never forced to run beyond the point of contact to recover your balance. If you're off-balance as you hit the ball, however, you'll need what's known as "recovery steps," and that will put you out of position for the next shot.

Basically, recovery steps are used to stop your forward momentum so you don't hurt yourself with an abrupt stop—so they *are* necessary at times. But many players use recovery steps on *every* shot, making it much more difficult to get back into position, and leaving much more court to cover than is necessary.

The idea is to get to the ball in plenty of time to stop your momentum at the point where you intend to contact the ball. Instead, many players time their run to intercept the ball just as it gets to where they plan to contact it. This means they're forced to run several steps beyond the point of contact to slow themselves. If you take three recovery steps it will take you three more steps just to get back to where you contacted the ball. That means the player who does not use recovery steps is six steps ahead of you. Those are six steps you can't afford. That's why professionals learn to slide to the ball on clay, because the tricky footing of the surface does not allow for quick stops and by sliding they can go full speed and yet still brake themselves so they aren't forced to go beyond the point of contact.

When you're forced to use recovery steps and your opponent is at the net you must either lob in order to buy more time so you can get back into position or you must try to end the point immediately by going for the outright winner. Curiously, these two shots are seldom attempted. If your opponent is at the baseline, a looping semi-lob is effective, since it also gives you time to recover, is relatively easy to control, and cannot be easily smashed away by your opponent.

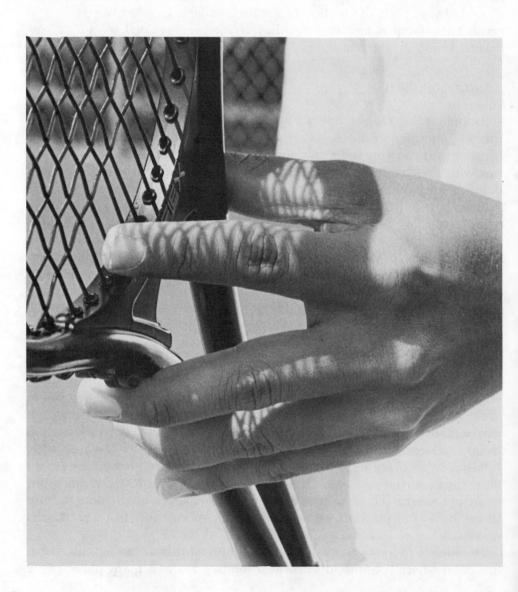

Fig. 34. The left hand is a vital part of racquet awareness. If you keep the index finger of your left hand lightly touching the strings, it will "tell" you where your racquet head is at all times. The fingertip control tells you the angle of the racquet head, which enables you to adjust the depth and direction of your shots.

3. THE USE OF THE LEFT HAND

The final ingredient to a good stroke and the key to self-correction is the use of the left hand (see Fig. 34). Basically, the left hand (for a right-handed player) has four functions:

1. To change grips
2. To rest your racquet hand
3. To keep the racquet head up
4. As a guide hand on the racquet

Using the Left Hand to Change Grips

It is impossible to show every player the correct backhand grip that's right for him. There is a total individuality to the grip. It changes from player to player because there are so many variables involved. For example, everyone's fingers are different lengths and their hands are constructed differently, and also there are many types, shapes, and sizes of racquet handles.

You will see dozens of books and thousands of pros, however, who teach that you can find the backhand grip by "placing the V between the thumb and the forefinger down the left edge of the handle." Or something like that. But that does not take into account round or oddly shaped racquet handles or the myriad variations of the human hand. That's why there's so much confusion. A player will be stuck with an improper grip for years and therefore be unable to present the racquet face to the ball without being forced to compensate by bending his wrist into some awkward and weak position.

That's the reason that in my recent years of teaching I haven't shown anyone the backhand grip. I prefer to train my students to adjust the grip with their left hands. I have a student set the racquet head up perpendicular to the ground with the left hand and hit several balls, adjusting the grip accordingly until it feels both strong *and* comfortable.

When changing to the backhand grip, never place the thumb behind the handle for added support. This severely limits your progress because it inhibits the rotation of your wrist necessary to execute many of the shots used by more advanced players. It also tends to make you poke at the ball. You'll tend to stick your elbow out toward the ball and use the elbow as the pivotal point of your swing—which is a great way to get tennis elbow. The pivotal point of your backhand stroke should be your shoulder, for very sound anatomical reasons. Your shoulder is a rollable or pivotal joint, while your elbow is a bendable joint. When you lead with your elbow instead of your shoulder you're asking your elbow to act as a rollable joint—that is, it rolls over, stretching ligaments and tendons designed only to bend. Before you know it you're wearing one of those little white support bands around your elbow. On ground strokes your thumb is basically a nonfunctional digit—it should simply be wrapped around the racquet handle.

Using the Left Hand to Relax the Racquet Hand Between Shots

Closely related to the grip change is the relaxation of the right hand between shots, because common sense will tell you that you can't change grips without releasing your grip on the racquet. Even more important, however, the left hand enables you to rest the right hand between shots (see Fig. 35a).

Figs. 35a-b. It is extremely important to use the left hand to completely relax the racquet hand (right hand). If you're having difficulty relaxing the right hand, work drills in which you completely remove the right hand from the grip between shots.

a.

Fig. 36a. A racquet is in balance when you have your left hand well up on the throat.

Fig. 36b. As your left hand moves down the throat, the racquet becomes "head heavy," often leading to a "wristy" slapping motion on ground strokes.

Many players use a "long intensity grip," which means they continue to grip very tightly long before they've hit the ball and long after. This creates undue muscle fatigue. Instead, a good player uses a "short intensity grip" that's loose between shots, working the racquet with the left hand. This keeps the right hand completely limp between shots and ready and able to supply power when it's time.

You may have difficulty remembering to use the left hand to "rest" between shots, so a little gimmick to use (in practice only) is to wipe your racquet hand on your shorts between every shot until you get comfortable with this technique.

Using the Left Hand to Keep the Racquet Head Up

A beginning or intermediate player tends to drop his racquet head down around his knees between shots because his hand gets tired holding the racquet up. If he'd use his left hand for support, though, his racquet hand would not get fatigued. Getting your left hand up toward the top of the handle with the index finger actually touching the strings is important for a balanced racquet (see Fig. 35b). You don't carry a long pole by grabbing it at one end with both hands. You put one hand farther up the pole to create a better balance. There's a tremendous amount of weight in the racquet head pulling it down, and if you have your left hand down next to your racquet hand, over the course of a match that racquet can begin to feel as if there's a lead weight at the end. That's when the wrist gets whippy and the shots begin to fly all over the place (see Figs. 36a-b).

Using the Left Hand as a Guide for the Racquet Face

The most important use of the left hand is as a guide for the racquet face. The left hand tells you how far from the body the racquet head is, how high or low it is, and how far back you've taken it, without looking at the racquet or taking your attention from the court, the ball, and the opponent—where it should be. The left hand tells the brain, which tells the racquet hand, what the angle of the racquet head is, and this bit of anatomical teamwork gets the ball over the net.

Some players are born with the ability to hit the ball in the center of the strings and some are not. Most are not. I've had a problem all my life with hitting the ball on the frame. I did experiments in which I put blacking on balls and painted the racquet white, and I'd color almost the entire frame black during the course of a set just from hitting the frame so much. But as soon as I began using the left hand this problem suddenly disappeared.

The left hand is also the key to correcting problems with direction, but this will be discussed later (see Chapter Seven).

Chapter Six
The Five Dimensions
of a Stroke

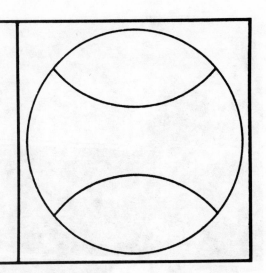

As you are mastering the physical problems of hitting a ball by mastering the three fundamentals of a sound stroke, you should also be developing your understanding of what to do *with* the ball. There are five basic things to think about when you hit a tennis ball. They are what I call "the five dimensions of a stroke": (1) Getting it in—get the ball over the net into your opponent's court any way you can; (2) Direction—gain control over whether you hit the ball left, right, crosscourt, or down the line; (3) Depth—be able not just to hit the ball to the opponent's baseline but to any depth, short, medium, or very deep. In other words, be able to *vary* depth; (4) Spin—you can perform miracles with spin. You can make a ball curve in or hop over your opponent's head. Control of spin separates the beginner from the advanced player; and (5) Speed—anybody can blast the ball but the good player can control the ball at any speed.

Practice is the time to develop your strokes—not during a match. When practicing you should follow a certain developmental progression for each stroke:

1. Getting it in
2. Direction
3. Depth
4. Spin
5. Speed

I don't mean to imply that you can't practice all five dimensions at the same time, because in fact many of these dimensions overlap, especially as you advance. But your *emphasis* should follow this order. In other words, concentrate on dimension 1, "Getting it in," until you can get it in most of the time, then concentrate on dimensions 2, 3, 4, and 5 in order.

A major stumbling block for most players is their inability to understand that tennis is a game of control, not power. Power or speed is the last stage in the development of a good tennis player. And even at this stage, the player must develop *controlled* power. Because power does not come from swinging harder but from better timing (which takes years to develop), and timing is the *ultimate control* of the racquet.

a.

b.

Figs. 37a-d. Sequences of an over-the-shoulder wrist flick. Learn to use this shot. It's often the only way to get the ball back. Note that on completion of the shot, the toes still point toward the back fence. In emergencies form is useless. If I had time to get set, I wouldn't need a wrist flick. Also, taking the racquet through high or low over the shoulder will determine the arc on the ball.

1. GETTING IT IN

To get the ball in the court, the first thing you must do is contact the ball. Beginners always take up their positions at the baselines as they see the pros do on TV and they seldom hit more than two balls in a row over the net in an hour. Most of their time is spent picking up balls, and then they complain that they never get enough exercise when they play tennis.

If this is your problem, come in closer and play mini-tennis (see Figs. 7 and 8). Develop some feel for contact area and learn to deal with the obstruction of the net and playing within a confined area. From there you can expand. But give yourself a chance to succeed. If you can't get the ball over the net, lower the net. If you can't get it back over the lowered net, hit back and forth over a line. But don't go through the frustration of taking your racquet all the way back and complicating what's already a difficult task. There is no form involved in just getting it in.

To get to a decent level in tennis, contrary to popular opinion, is not that difficult. To get really good—yes, that's a difficult job. But just to have some reasonable success there is no real difficulty. Of course, if you think you

c.

d.

should be on the pro tour in two years and you play twice a week, then you're just not being realistic. But you can play a decent game without a lot of horrible frustration if you'd just forget about hitting the perfect shot and instead concentrate on just getting it in.

That's why tennis is often much harder for the good athlete in the beginning than the nonathlete. An athlete wants to play like Connors in two weeks and ends up overhitting and trying to look good. In other words, he tries to do things he can't do right away and becomes frustrated.

Many of my beginning students will sigh in relief when I tell them it's all right to try anything they want to get the ball over the net. One of my first drills, in fact, with beginning women who cannot hit an overhead is simply to have them run back and flip the ball back over their heads (see Figs. 37a-d), because many beginning women have a built-in weak, floppy wrist. So this flipping motion is quite natural for them and also very effective.

Also, I encourage squash or racquetball players to take those natural wrist shots and use them whenever they can in tennis. A squash player can handle emergencies quite nicely, though he has trouble with a medium-paced ball right down the middle. What I'm suggesting is that you take your natural strength and make it into an effective shot.

Figs. 38a-b. On the backhand wrist flick, use a forehand grip. Your muscles are stronger for this type of shot with a forehand grip.

a.

b.

Take what you *can* do and develop it into a strength. For example, the wrist flick is a very natural thing. There isn't a person in the world who starts playing tennis with a naturally "locked" wrist. So if you're extended to the end of your reach (see Figs. 38a-b) or the ball gets behind you by all means, do what comes naturally—flick the wrist! Form won't help you in those situations, and besides, that's what Borg or Connors would do. The difference is that unlike a beginner, Connors does not find himself in that situation on nearly every shot.

2. DIRECTION

You can't be satisfied forever, though, with just getting the ball over the net. Your goal should be to have the ability to hit to any part of the court, but especially to the seven target zones—the two deep corners, the two side T's, the two dropshot areas (or drop volley areas), and down the middle. The fundamental tools for learning to hit the ball where you want are mini-tennis and understanding the use of the left hand.

3. DEPTH

Most players think depth means hitting the ball deep in the court, so that the ball lands just inside the baseline. But just as there are many depths in a swimming pool, there are also many depths on a tennis court. There are many times when you don't want to hit the baseline. For instance, you may want to hit short in order to bring a good ground-stroker into the net or to move a slow player around. Or if you aim for the baseline when your opponent is at the net you may never see the ball again, because that's often a setup for a player at the net. The idea is to make a player at the net play a low shot so he's forced to arc the ball over the net.

You don't hit the ball deeper by swinging harder, which is a common misconception. Another misconception is that a good shot skims just a few inches over the net. In fact, a pro tries to clear the net by three to seven feet on normal ground strokes—three on fast courts, seven on very slow (see Fig. 39). This fact usually comes as a big surprise to most club players.

There is a direct relationship, however, between clearance of the net and depth. A line drive that just skims the net often falls short, and, more often than not, balls aimed three to six inches over the net never make it over at all. It's not how close you come to the net that's important, it's where the ball lands. A ball that clears the net by six feet if it has any speed at all *must* land deep in the court. So it follows, logically, that you can add depth simply by hitting the ball higher over the net.

How to Vary Depth

Perhaps the easiest way to increase depth is by opening up the angle of your racquet face with the left hand. To hit shorter, close your racquet face.

Another way of lengthening depth is by lengthening your contact area. Contact area is defined as the area in which the racquet and ball are in contact with each other, and lengthening or shortening the contact area is one way of lengthening or shortening depth. Your contact area can be

Fig. 39. An excellent gimmick to learn to hit deeper is to fix one net above another net. This means that minimum clearance of the ball over the actual net must be 3 feet. Professionals, when rallying from baseline to baseline, aim for a net clearance of between 3 and 7 feet. Beginners usually try to "skim" the net.

lengthened, then, by pushing forward with your palm (and, thus, the racquet face) through the contact area.

The best way to lengthen contact area is to stand with your feet a reasonable distance apart and *bend your knees*. When you bend your knees the center of gravity lowers, thereby creating better balance. And if you widen your base while bending your knees, you create a potentially longer contact area. This enables you to push forward a longer distance with your palm through the contact area without losing your balance. Conversely, if you stand straight up or with your feet close together, you limit your contact area, which results in a shot that is nothing more than a slap.

Hitting with an open stance also tends to shorten the contact area. Your balance zone with an open stance is only the length of your foot, and therefore a player who hits a forehand or backhand with his body facing the net often hits short because he has a very limited potential contact area.

I'm not advocating hitting every shot with a closed stance, but the great open-stance forehand players like Laver and Borg learned to bend way down to increase their potential contact and concentrated hitting with an elongated contact area—in other words, pushing the palm forward through the ball.

You should basically avoid hitting open-stance backhands, because the forearm is not usually strong enough on a backhand to maintain an elongated contact area. However, sometimes it is necessary; for example, when the ball is hit directly at you and you don't have time to move. In those cases, remember to use minimum potential (see Chapter Two, "Minimum Potential").

Drill for varying depth

Once you have the basis for ball control—"getting it in" and "direction"—try the three-ball target drill. You and a friend space three balls evenly across the alley at the service lines and see who can hit the opponent's ball first. The purpose is to teach you to vary depth. Hit one short, then one long, until you get the range.

Then move to the baseline in the alley for full depth. Put a racquet cover at the baseline and three balls at the service line and hit every other ball at a different target. Don't be concerned if your ball goes out at the baseline. This is a drill to get a feel for depth.

4. SPIN

A more advanced technique for varying depth is through the use of spin. As I mentioned before, there are only two things that cause a ball to land in the court—gravity and spin. Beginners use gravity to make the ball literally "fall" into the court. If they want the ball to land deeper they hit it harder. Advanced players use spin.

Spin creates friction with the air, and friction slows an object down by creating a "drag" or resistance. It's the difference between skiing on powdery snow and skiing on ice. The ice gives very little resistance and the skier flies uncontrollably down the hill. Without spin the ball flies out of control. If you add spin you slow the ball down—you add control. Less spin gives less control; more spin, more control. That's why the pros can hit so hard and keep the ball in. They utilize spin.

Spin opens up a whole new world of creativity. You can hit harder, more difficult angles (for example, you can't hit effective side-T shots from the baseline without spin) and you can vary depth. More spin gives more drag and less depth; less spin gives less drag and more depth.

Knowing the results of different spins enables you to better exploit your opponent's weaknesses. A topspin bounces high, and most players hate a high ball to their backhand. A backspin bounces low and therefore must be hit up to clear the net, and a ball being hit up is more easily volleyed away (see Chapter Fifteen, "The D-N-O Theory").

When explaining how to hit spin I prefer not to go through any elaborate scientific explanations of vector forces. I've found those scientific explanations are often confusing for students. So let's keep it simple. In most cases, when trying to hit a topspin, swing from low to high and finish with the racquet on edge—that is, perpendicular to the ground (see Fig. 40). If the racquet face finishes open to the sky, you will hit backspin.

Perhaps the key ingredient to hitting spin is a *firm but flexible* wrist. Gone are the days of "racquet back—flat groundstrokes." This is the age of spin. It's important to realize the range of rotation the wrist must go through in order to hit successful spin. In other words, the palm must rotate upward for a backspin forehand. And for a backspin backhand the knuckles rotate upward. There's no way to hit a backspin ground stroke unless you rotate the wrist and racquet face to an open position. Or, if you're starting with a completely open racquet face, to hit a topspin you'll have to rotate the wrist in the opposite direction.

There are pros who advocate putting your thumb up the back of the handle for a firm "locked" wrist. But this makes it impossible to hit shots

Fig. 40. A good checkpoint on the topspin ground strokes is to notice if your racquet finishes on edge (or perpendicular to the ground) in front of your body.

such as a dropshot, which demand a full rotation of the wrist to properly execute. An iron-locked wrist is neither natural nor correct. You need that freedom of movement. Instead, the proper technique to achieve a firm but flexible wrist is to tighten the bottom three fingers of the hitting hand.

5. SPEED

The last element of the ground-stroke progression is speed. But speed does not mean just hitting the ball hard. It means *all* speeds. Can you hit the ball slow and easy as well as hard and fast? In order to be a good tennis player you must be able to do both. There are many times in a match when a slow-hit ball is the *best* shot—even on a passing shot.

It may feel great to hit the ball hard, but tennis is a game of restrictions imposed upon you by lines, obstacles (the net), and an opponent, who is trying to make the restrictions and obstacles that much greater. That's why I emphasize the phrase "racquet preparation" rather than "racquet back." The only purpose of a bigger backswing is to hit the ball harder. I don't want speed to be a factor in the beginning until a player can handle speed.

Experiencing the Two Extremes

An excellent drill to learn to control speed is to experience the two extremes. First hit the ball for the first twenty minutes as hard as you can. Just nail it—gamble completely on every shot. Then for the next twenty minutes hit everything with total touch and placement. This drill impresses upon you the slim possibilities of getting the ball in if you hit it as hard as you can. Also, after experimenting with these two extremes, the medium-paced, steady shot seems simple.

Phase Three
How to Be Your Own Coach
Part II: Simplicity Checkpoints

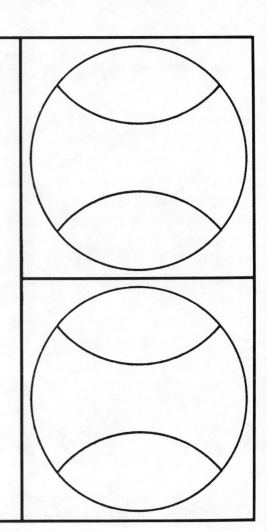

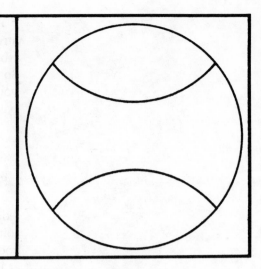

Chapter Seven
Types of Simplicity
Checkpoints

Simplicity checkpoints are designed to enable you to correct the particular problems that you're having with strokes. There are simplicity checkpoints to use during a match and simplicity checkpoints to use during practice.

1. SIMPLICITY CHECKPOINTS DURING A MATCH

The next phase of self-coaching is the development of simplicity checkpoints that you can use in a match situation when your strokes are beginning to desert you. Simplicity checkpoints are simple pieces of advice you can give yourself as a guide to correct your stroke problems.

Your approach to self-coaching during a match must be very simple, or you'll only confuse yourself. Before you know it, nothing will be going over the net. You don't want to be out on the court during a match trying to learn how to hit a backhand volley. That's for your practice sessions. You should concern yourself only with what you can do to correct your errors and have a few checkpoints you can fall back on if one of your strokes begins to falter.

Simplicity checkpoints for match situations are inevitably something each individual must develop personally. By the use of a number of simplicity checkpoints I offer to develop strokes in practice situations, a player should be able to find one or two "catch words" that can serve as a checkpoint when a specific stroke gives him trouble in a match.

Specific problems with a stroke are usually chronic—they show up over and over again. And they're likely to show up most in pressure situations. That's when a simplicity checkpoint developed by practicing on that chronic problem can come in very handy.

Some of my own personal checkpoints have pulled me through one emergency after another. On the forehand I think about "squeezing the bottom three fingers" to reduce my tendency to slap at the ball. On the backhand I think "left hand." On the serve I think "hit up" because I'm not very tall and I tend to hit into the net when pressured. And on passing shots I try to "relax" because passing shots are always pressure situations.

Remember, in a match forget about how your strokes look. Developing strokes is a matter of practice—a great topspin backhand takes years of hard work and talent. In other words, you've got the strokes you showed up with. So concentrate during a match on the simplicity checkpoints that work for you and on the three fundamentals of sound stroking—contact area, balance, and the use of the left hand.

2. SIMPLICITY CHECKPOINTS DURING PRACTICE

I don't believe in teaching students exactly how to hit a ball. If you want someone to show you the so-called classic strokes, there are a hundred books out there. But let me stress this—*there is no right way to hit a ball.* Look at Borg or Connors or McEnroe. None of them has truly classic strokes. But there are certain common characteristics to every good stroke, and you can use them as checkpoints to improve your strokes.

The basic assumption of self-correction is that there is something to correct. If your game is going great you don't need to coach yourself. If you don't like the results you're getting, however, then you must correct the cause of those bad results.

Most players are unaware of what happens when they play. They hit the ball and they're either satisfied or frustrated with the result. They don't bother to analyze the result that occurred. The problem is that most players, when practicing, only watch where the ball landed on the first bounce. The real secret to ball control, however, is where the ball lands on the *second* bounce, because that's the spot, theoretically, where your opponent will be, and ball control ultimately means control of your opponent.

3. THE SECOND-BOUNCE THEORY

The second-bounce theory is useful when practicing side-T shots, dropshots, and the serve. If you want to hit an effective ground stroke to a side T, the second bounce should land outside the doubles alley, because the purpose of a side-T shot should be to pull your opponent off the court (see Diagram 4a).

On your dropshot, the second bounce, at worst, should land inside the service line, and ideally the ball should bounce three times inside the service box (see Diagram 4b). The important thing, however, on your dropshot, is making the second bounce land as close as possible to the first bounce. This is accomplished with backspin (there is no such thing as a topspin dropshot) and arc. A good dropshot will clear the net by three to five feet. Anything higher will give your opponent too much time to get to the ball. And, if you hit the ball with too low an arc, the second bounce will probably land too deep in the court. If you're extremely close to the net, however, you can lower the arc.

The second-bounce theory is helpful on the serve, too. For example, on a slice serve wide to the deuce court, the second bounce should land outside the doubles alley, and a topspin serve should hit the fence before the second bounce (see Diagram 4c).

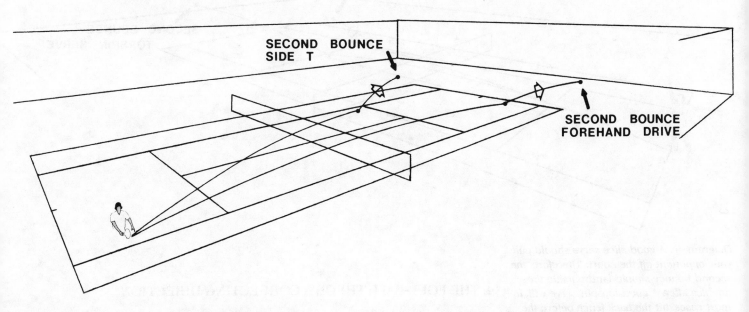

SECOND BOUNCE SIDE T

SECOND BOUNCE FOREHAND DRIVE

Diagram 4a. The ball lands outside the doubles alley on the second bounce when you hit an effective ground stroke to a side T. On a well-hit forehand drive, the ball should land well beyond the base line on the second bounce.

Diagram 4b. On a well-hit dropshot, the ball should bounce three times inside the service box.

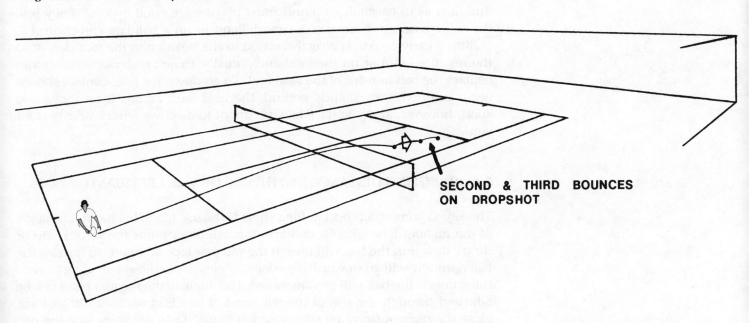

SECOND & THIRD BOUNCES ON DROPSHOT

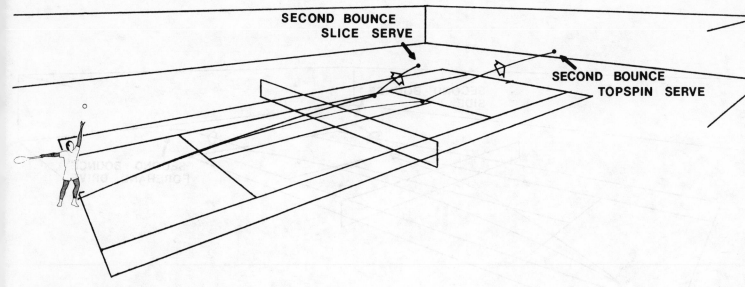

SECOND BOUNCE SLICE SERVE

SECOND BOUNCE TOPSPIN SERVE

Diagram 4c. A good slice serve should pull your opponent off the court. Therefore, the second bounce should land outside the doubles alley. A good topspin serve will, in most cases, hit the back fence before the second bounce. Remember, if you know where the ball will land on the second bounce, then you know where your opponent will be, which means that you can then control your opponent's position.

4. THE FOUL-BALL THEORY: CORRECTING DIRECTION

The first point to remember is that there are only four basic errors in tennis: the ball goes too far to the right, or too far to the left, or too long, or too short (into the net).

The average player's conception of how to change the direction to the left or right (crosscourt or down the line) is to change the direction of his body and hit the ball exactly the same—which is fine if he wants to let his opponent know where he's hitting the ball every time. Instead, the direction of the ball should be determined by whether you contact the ball "early" or "late" (see Figs. 41a-c). This is the so-called "foul-ball" theory. In baseball if you're a right-handed batter and you hit the ball too late, the ball will go foul down the right-field line; if you hit the ball too early, it will go foul down the left-field line. And, just as in baseball, in tennis most players are "pull hitters." They pull the ball crosscourt because it's very difficult to hit a ball late and control it.

Hitting early or late is directly related to the position of the foot closest to the net (the left foot on the forehand). Ideally, to go crosscourt you should contact the ball in front of the lead foot. To go down the line, contact should occur even with, or slightly behind, the lead foot. Tennis is an individual sport, however, and you have to experiment to discover what works best for you.

5. CORRECTING DISTANCE BY THE USE OF THE LEFT HAND

The key to correcting short or long shots is the use of the left hand. The angle of the racquet face when it contacts the ball determines the vertical (up or down) direction the ball will take. If the racquet face is "open" to the sky, the ball naturally will go upward; if the face is "closed" to the sky (angling toward the ground), the ball will go downward. The angle of the racquet head can be adjusted through the use of the left hand. If you find yourself hitting long, close the racquet face a bit with your left hand. If you're hitting into the net, then open the racquet face with the left hand.

Fig. 41a. The direction of the ball is not determined by the position of the body but by the point of contact. To hit crosscourt, contact the ball early.

To correct your mistakes you must go through some trial and error and adjustment. If you make a mistake, don't hit two consecutive balls long or two consecutive balls short. Hit one long and one short by adjusting with the left hand until you zero in on the proper depth. Remember, every mistake in depth you make on your forehand or backhand is the fault of your left hand. So put your mind in your left hand.

Think left hand!

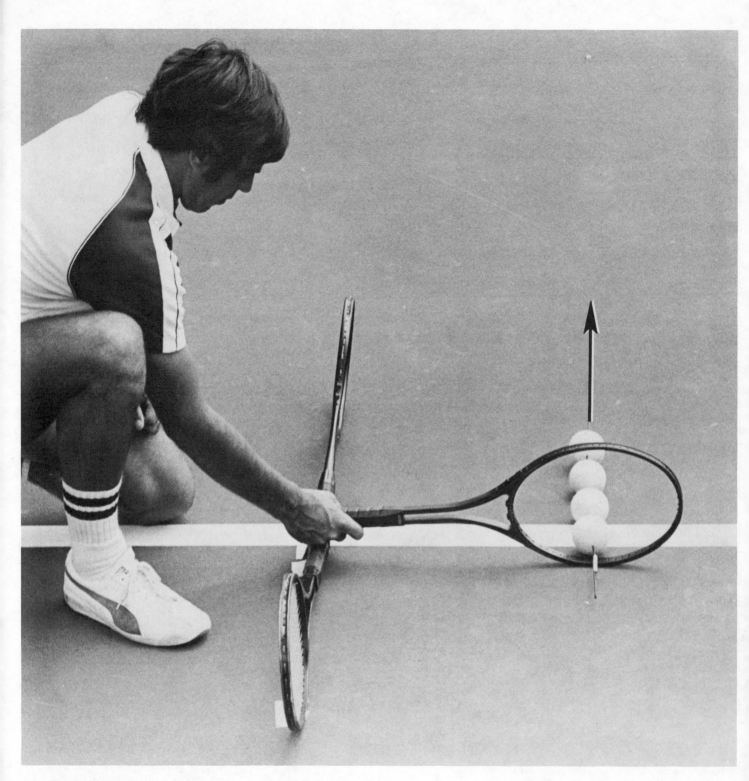

Fig. 41b. When you contact the ball in line with your body, the direction of the ball will be down the center.

Fig. 41c. To hit down the line, contact the ball late. Of course, if you contact the ball too late, the ball will go out, wide, down the line. If you contact the ball too early, it will go out, wide, crosscourt.

Chapter Eight
Simplicity Checkpoints for Ground Strokes

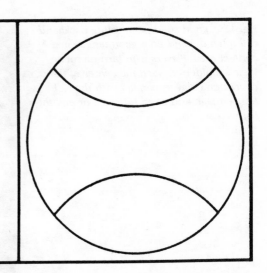

Many times a player will mishit a shot, then look down at his racquet as if to say, "How could you do this to me?" Once you begin to realize, however, what's actually happening when you mishit a shot you can begin to correct the real cause of the trouble—you!

The fundamentals for both the forehand and the backhand are contact area, balance, and the use of the left hand. So when I teach ground strokes I never separate the forehand from the backhand (see Fig. 42). What you learn on the forehand you just flip over to the backhand side, because they're both ground strokes and the basic understanding of what to do is the same. You must hit crosscourt shots, down-the-line shots, dropshots, lobs—you must do everything from both sides. And if you have a problem on one side you usually have it on the other as well. If you take too much of a backswing you'll usually do it on both sides, and if you flip your wrist over on the forehand you'll usually flip it over on the backhand as well. So the correction is usually the same for the forehand and backhand.

Before I go on to explain the checkpoints, I'd like to describe the different grips you use.

First there is the "Eastern Forehand" (the "shake hands grip"). Put your palm flat against the strings and slide the palm down the shaft to the handle to get this grip (see Fig. 43a).

Next is the "Western Forehand" (the "frying-pan grip"). Here the palm of the hand is further under the racquet. A way of obtaining the Western grip is to first put the racquet flat on the ground and then pick it up.

And last there is the "Continental" (the "hammer grip"). The hand is on top of the racquet and it is held just as if you were going to hammer a nail with the edge of the racquet (see Fig. 44).

1. WHY CHANGE GRIPS?

There's only one thing that significantly differs from backhand to forehand, and that is the grip. If you ask a hundred people why they change grips to hit a backhand, seventy-five will say their pro told them to do it and the other

Fig. 42. A good solid penetrating backhand will often depend on a good lengthened contact area. Players who turn or rotate their shoulders toward the center of the court don't stay in contact with the ball long enough and often hit short or pull the ball crosscourt.

twenty-five will say they read it somewhere. They have virtually no personal understanding of why they should change grips.

The reason you change from an Eastern or Western Forehand to a conventional Eastern Backhand grip to hit a backhand is common sense—so you can have the ability to present the racquet face flat to the ball *and* have a firm wrist at the same time. If you don't change grips for a backhand and you try to present a flat racquet face to the ball, then your wrist will be contorted in some strange position. Or, if you keep a firm wrist, the racquet face, with a forehand grip, will be pointing to the sky and the ball will go where the racquet face is pointed (see Figs. 43a-b and 45a-b).

If you use a Continental grip for ground strokes you do not need to change grips. But there are two serious disadvantages in using a Continental grip to hit and that's why I don't recommend it. First of all, to hit high-bouncing balls to your forehand, you must contort your wrist into a very awkward and weak position, making it very difficult to generate power unless you've got great strength in your wrists. Second, on low-bouncing balls, in order to present the racquet face flat to the ball on the forehand, you must hit with a straight arm. And that's one of the easiest ways to develop tennis elbow.

2. CHECKPOINTS FOR GROUND STROKES

The principal checkpoints for any ground stroke are, of course, the fundamentals of good stroking: (1) contact area, (2) balance, and (3) the use of the left hand.

Correcting the Contact Area

Perhaps the major problem most players develop on their ground strokes is the overworking of the racquet head. The racquet head seems to be flying all over the place—whipping over the shoulder, slapping at the ball, flopping all around in the backswing (see Figs. 46a-b and 47). To check this problem:

1. Think "fast feet, slow arm." Pretend your arm is in a slow-motion picture and concentrate on a fluid controlled swing.
2. Squeeze tightly with the last three fingers on the racquet hand as you hit. This creates a firm wrist and eliminates the slapping motion of the racquet.
3. Freeze at the end of the stroke to check your finish. Can you see the racquet between you and the ball, or has it wrapped back around your shoulder?
4. When you hit, think "palm forward" on the forehand and "knuckles forward" on the backhand. This helps increase your awareness of contact area.
5. Get a visual image of hitting through four balls. I often have students take a racquet without strings and swing through four balls "strung" together on a coat hanger so they can get a mental picture of hitting through the ball (see Figs. 48a-d).

Fig. 43a. The conventional Eastern forehand grip. Many of the top players in the world today, however, use a semi-Western or Western forehand grip.

Fig. 43b. A backhand shot with a forehand grip. The weak, contorted position of the wrist points out the obvious reason why a grip change is necessary.

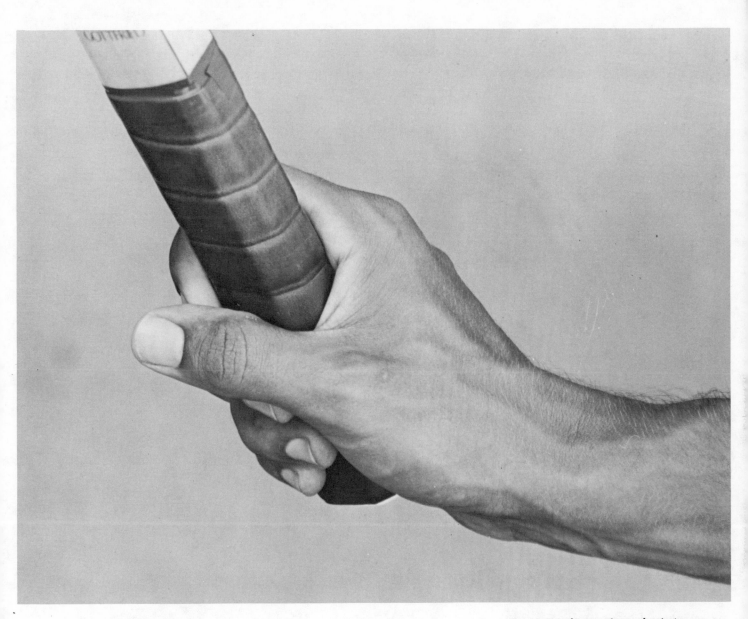

Fig. 44. For the Continental grip (sometimes referred to as the hammer grip), the hand is placed on top of the racquet handle. The Continental grip is the proper grip to use on both the serve and the volley.

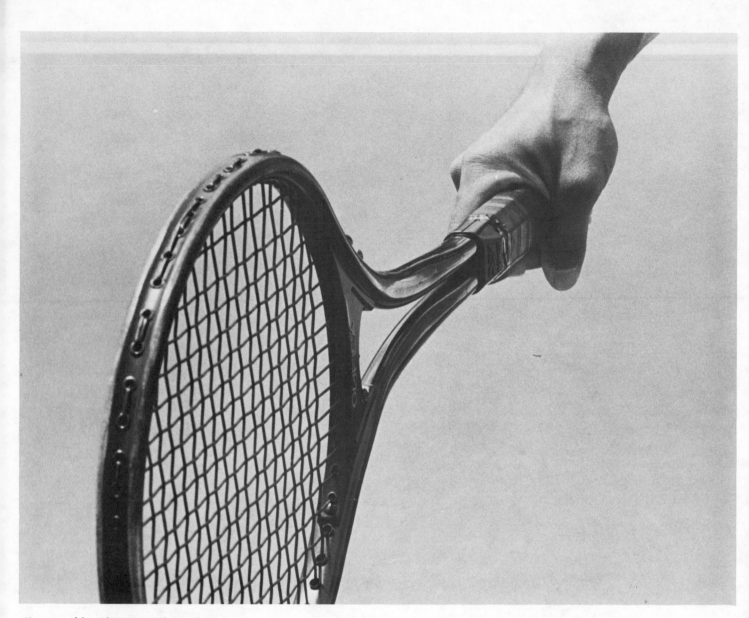

Fig. 45a. Although it varies from player to player, this is the conventional backhand grip.

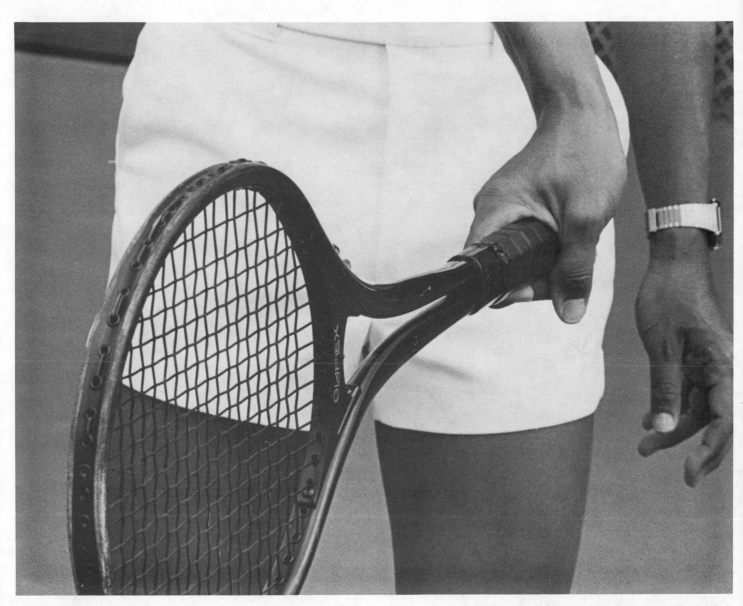

Fig. 45b. A forehand ground stroke with a backhand grip. You contort the wrist into an unnatural and weak position, leading to possible injury and weak shots.

a.

b.

Figs. 46a-b. Don't get too elaborate with the follow-through. Avoid wrapping the racquet around your stomach or around your neck. Let your hand flow freely forward and the follow-through will take care of itself.

Fig. 47. Many players step across their bodies into the court after they hit. This causes the racquet face to follow a circular or slapping motion. This unnecessary step may also cause you to be out of position for the next shot.

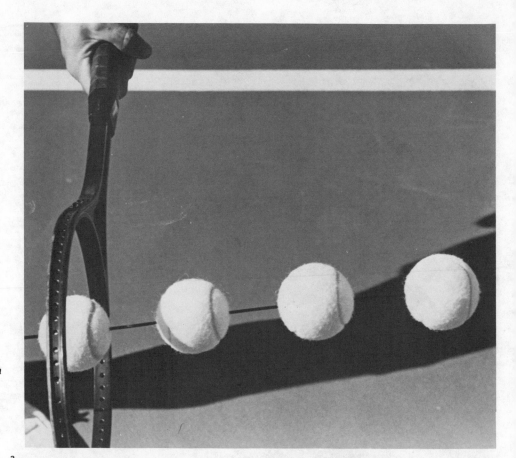
a.

Figs. 48a-d. Don't "slap" at the ball. To gain depth and control, think about hitting through four balls. Note that the wrist and racquet head stay in the same line throughout the contact area. The racquet head is an extension of the hand. Work them together.

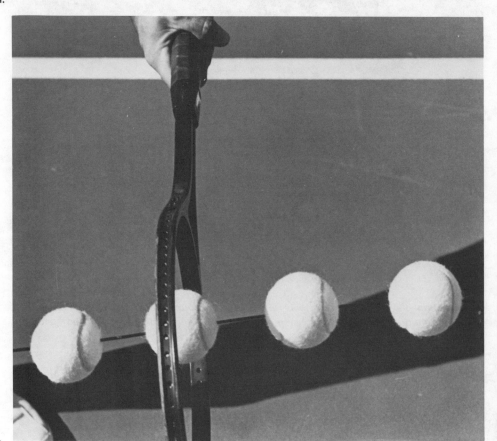
b.

c.

d.

a. b.

Figs. 49a-b. You find "flamingos" all over the world. Some people like to hit the flamingo shot off the front foot, others off the back foot.

Correcting Balance

1. Make sure your weight is on your lead foot as you hit, that is, the left foot for the forehand and the right foot for the backhand. Don't be a "flamingo" (see Figs. 49a-b).
2. After you hit, freeze and see if you can place your racquet on the ground between your feet (see Fig. 31). This will indicate if your feet are properly spaced, and by forcing yourself to stop, you can check any unnecessary use of recovery steps.

Checking for the Use of the Left Hand

In practice, wipe your racquet hand on your shorts between each shot to ensure that the racquet is in the left hand. Remember, all mistakes on the ground strokes are the fault of the left hand. Think left hand!

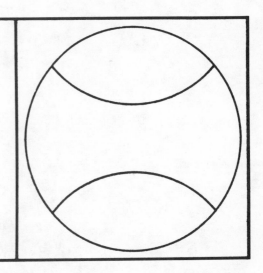

Chapter Nine
Simplicity Checkpoints for the Volley

1. POSSIBLE MISUNDERSTANDINGS

There are some common phrases used in connection with the volley which I believe can be too easily misinterpreted. One of them is "punching the volley" and the other is "hitting the ball as far out in front of you as possible."

Many people's conception of a punch involves straightening the arm, and doing this on the forehand volley is, I believe, the single most detrimental movement when hitting this stroke. An effective forehand volley covers only a distance of six to ten inches and is hit with an arm going from a bent to bent position. You want minimal racquet motion on the volley, and on a "punch," the racquet motion is often too long. The player who tries to contact the ball too far in front, who straightens his arm prematurely, will be unable to adjust to anything unexpected—to wind, to mishits, to miscalculations. He loses his potential for power, because he loses the potential to accelerate through the ball.

Another widespread misconception is that you should change your grip back and forth for a backhand and forehand volley. There is seldom time for such adjustments on a normal-paced ball hit from the baseline or when two players are at the net volleying at close range, which often happens in doubles.

One of the few things I will insist on in this book is that all volleys must be hit with a Continental grip (see Fig. 44). The Continental grip is the only grip that enables you (on both a backhand and forehand) to simultaneously have a firm wrist *and* an open racquet face—the two key elements for a good volley.

2. COURT POSITIONING ON VOLLEYS

Volleys should only be hit from three places on the court:

1. The Ideal Volley Position, or IVP, is halfway between the net and the service line. It is ideal because you can get back and cover a lob from that position and yet still prevent the opponent from getting the ball down at your feet.
2. The Defensive Volley Position, or DVP, is around the service line. The only time you should hit a volley from here is on the first volley when serving and volleying. You don't go for winners from the DVP because you're usually not in the position to hit side-T angles, which means

it's difficult to put the ball away. Also, the greater distance to your opponent's baseline allows him plenty of time to get to the ball.

3. The Best Volley Position, or BVP, is right on top of the net. You should only volley this close to the net if the ball is a setup and you can move up and put it away. If you station yourself in the BVP as a matter of course, a smart opponent will lob on every shot, since you're completely vulnerable to even a mediocre lob.

3. CHECKPOINTS FOR THE VOLLEY

Racquet Face Open

When volleying, your racquet face must be open. The Continental grip allows you to have both a firm wrist and an open racquet face. Why do you want an open racquet face? To create backspin. Why do you want backspin? Because it's your control spin, and the volley, contrary to popular belief, is not a big slam-bang shot. It is a control shot.

If you want to develop control of your volley, develop spin. Spin causes friction with the air. More spin causes more friction, and that causes the ball to drop into the court sooner. That is the basic principle for controlling depth. Also, an open racquet face is critical when hitting low volleys. The volley cannot be a straight-line shot if the ball is hit from anywhere below the net. If the ball is low you must be able to put arc on the ball in order to clear the net.

To hit deep, use less spin; to hit short, use more spin. This is a very simple approach, and though hitting backspin on your volleys is sometimes a difficult concept to learn initially, like anything else, as you learn the "feel" of it you learn to adjust, adding a bit more or less spin to get the result you desire. I want you to think long-term—so stick with it. There's a future in this concept.

The only other way to adjust the depth on your volleys is to hit harder or softer, which is a very unpredictable method. The advantage of spin as opposed to speed is that the speed with which you can hit the ball differs every day because of many reasons, including biorhythms (some days you come out feeling fantastic and you can really pound the ball), different altitudes, and different balls. To try to adjust distance by how hard you hit the ball is just not practical. Whether you like it or not, the speed of the ball will change from day to day, but spin is your old reliable. Once you master backspin you can add or reduce spin consciously without other factors affecting the result.

Think "Catch"

In order to learn backspin you must learn to get "under the ball." That's why I teach the volley as a "catch" (see Figs. 50a-b). If you want to catch a ball you don't slap at it, you get under it. "Catch" is a preliminary thought process that enables you to remember to maintain an open racquet face while volleying. Usually, if your volley falls apart, you'll start dumping the ball into the net. If you think "catch" it will help you get under the ball, put a good arc on it, and get it over the net.

Think catch!

Fig. 50a. Think catch. By doing so, the racquet is presented open. The open racquet face automatically creates backspin, which is the foundation of a solid volley.

Fig. 50b. The open racquet face enables the student to think of "catching" the ball. The "catching" racquet (with a fishnet) has been one of PBI's most successful gimmicks to teach people how to volley. The volley is not a "punch." It's motion is more similar to a "catch."

Fig. 51a. Keep your wrist and racquet head together for an effective volley.

Fig. 51b. If you exaggerate the "laid-back" wrist position, you'll have difficulty volleying crosscourt and put great strain on your wrist.

Fig. 51c. If you let your racquet head get ahead of your wrist, you'll tend to slap at the ball and have trouble hitting down the line.

Wrist and Racquet Head Together

The ball will go exactly where your strings are pointing. In other words, if you present the racquet face in a certain direction, the ball will always go there. If the wrist and racquet head are both parallel to the net at point of contact, the ball will go directly back across the net, which is to say down the line. If the racquet head is slightly ahead of the wrist, the ball will go crosscourt. It's that simple. So to correct problems of direction on the volley, use the checkpoint "wrist and racquet head together" and note where your racquet strings are pointing after you hit the ball (see Figs. 51a-c). (Note: Direction is not so easily calculated on ground strokes, because to hit down the line you must contact the ball behind your lead foot, but volleys are usually hit in front no matter what their direction. This one small difference is critical.)

The player who lets his racquet head get ahead of his wrist will usually volley the ball down the center when he wants to go down the line. This is a critical bit of misdirection, because when you're in trouble you should volley down the line. A crosscourt volley (unless you can hit an outright winner) opens up the entire court for the opponent to hit into, and to properly cover the court you will have to shift to the opposite side of the center line to cut down your opponent's angles. If you're in trouble you usually don't have time for such adjustments, which means you're wide open for even mediocre passing shots.

Maintain a Firm Wrist

If you don't maintain a firm wrist on your volleys, a hard-hit ball will often force the racquet face to pop open, which will cause the ball to pop up. Or the racquet will sometimes turn in your hand. This gives players, especially women, the feeling that the ball is stronger than they are because they can't hang onto the racquet. This helps create the fear that so many players have at the net. It's a definite psychological blow when someone knocks your racquet loose. You begin to think, "Geez, I've got no business at the net."

To firm up the wrist, squeeze the bottom three fingers of the racquet hand.

Keep the Racquet Head Up

This is especially helpful if your volleys are falling short. If your racquet head is up, you'll have a firmer wrist and you'll tend to play the ball higher than normal. Anytime you can play the ball higher it increases your chances of getting the ball over the net, and if you drop your racquet head you will inevitably hit the ball at a lower position. This often means the difference between taking the ball above or below the level of the net. With this simple adjustment, you will have gone from a defensive to an offensive position. And that's the difference between winning and losing.

Minimize the Backswing and Follow-through

What is the purpose of the backswing? To add power—but that's not your need when volleying. The volley is a controlled directional shot. If you follow through, the racquet head flies ahead of your wrist and you decrease your potential to go down the line.

Fig. 52a. The six stages for developing a good volley. Stage 1—hold your racquet as high on the throat as possible, let the ball hit the open racquet face, and catch it in your left hand.

Fig. 52b. Stage 2—hit the ball back to tosser. The tosser should check for open racquet face and minimum racquet movement.

c.

d.

Fig. 52c. Stage 3—hold racket halfway down the handle. Repeat Stage 1 (catch).

Fig. 52d. Stage 4—hold racquet halfway down the handle. Repeat Stage 2 (hit).

Fig. 52e. Stage 5—hold the racquet at the end. Repeat Stage 1 (catch).

Fig. 52f. Stage 6—take full grip and repeat Stage 2 (hit).

Fig. 52g. On the backhand volley, start at Stage 6—hold the racquet normally and volley back. The same checkpoints apply as on the forehand volley—open racquet face, backspin, and minimal motion.

Keep the Volley Compact

If you get stretched too far out front or to the side, your arm will be *prematurely straightened* prior to contact. This means you've eliminated any potential for necessary adjustments due to wind or strange spins. Most important, you have eliminated the potential to lengthen your contact area, and to accelerate or "explode" within the contact area, which enables you to increase your power without taking a bigger swing. And different volleys have different contact areas. On a DVP volley, a volley taken around the service line, you should lengthen the contact area, because the ball must travel a greater distance to land at the opponent's baseline than on a normal volley taken at the net. Whereas on a ball hit very hard directly at you, when you're right on top of the net, you need only a minimal contact area—just block the ball.

A good way to develop a compact volley style is to do the six-stage volley practice shown in Figs. 52a-g.

Keep a Two-ball Space Between Your Elbow and Stomach

This is particularly important for forehand volleys, because the tendency is to let the right elbow get behind the right hip, in which case the stroke gets "cramped" and your power zone is eliminated.

a.

Figs. 53a-c. As you move to higher levels of tennis, the players hit harder and more accurate passing shots. So get in the habit of using the crossover step. The increased reach can improve the range of your volley by one whole racquet length. Lazy volleyers tend to move only the foot closest to the ball, greatly reducing their offensive position at the net.

Keep a Bent Arm (on Forehand Volleys)

A volley is only a six- to ten-inch stroke, depending on the length of your arm and other variables. If you straighten your arm in a "punching" motion you're doing too much—the potential for mishits and misdirection increases as the length of your swing increases.

Turn Sideways

Turning sideways when volleying is related to the so-called "crossover" or "cross-in" step. When a player crosses his left foot over his right foot on a forehand volley (right to left on the backhand) it increases his reach by one full racquet length (see Figs. 53a-c).

b.

c.

Chapter Ten
Simplicity Checkpoints for the Serve

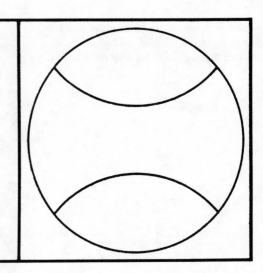

1. YOU'RE ONLY AS GOOD AS YOUR SECOND SERVE

Would you rather buy a car that goes 100 mph and has lousy brakes or one that goes 50 mph and has great brakes? Then why do so many players pound their first serve 100 mph and then dink the second one in? Remember, *you're only as good a player as your second serve.* That statement may hurt, but it's true. You've got to develop a dependable second serve, and the quickest way to do that is to stop putting so much pressure on your second serve by getting the first one in. As soon as you miss your first serve you're often in a mental emergency situation, and the idea is to avoid emergencies at all costs. So, slow down your first serve to the point where you have control over the ball *and* your body (see Fig. 54).

Your second serve is not just a slower version of your first serve, because that implies you're depending on gravity to make the ball "fall" into the service box. And the use of gravity is, as you recall, a beginner's technique. Instead, use spin. Spin slows the ball down by creating friction with the air, and you can control spin under pressure much more easily than you can control speed. With spin you can maintain the same service rhythm and the same arm speed on every serve and still slow the ball down and make it drop into the service box when you need it most.

You should adjust your serve according to how your opponent likes to hit his returns. First, determine the amount of his backswing by the distance he takes the racquet away from his body. If he takes the racquet back wide, serve into him or at him. If he has a compact swing, serve wide. Second, notice what types of spin your opponent can hit. If he can only hit backspin on the backhand side, then you should concentrate on moving into the net, because he will tend to float the ball or chip it short. Third, hit a high-kicking serve against a two-hander, because he is not as comfortable reaching up (see Fig. 55). (The most effective serve, however, against a two-hander is a lefty's slice serve, because the ball slides away from his already limited reach.) Fourth, against someone who runs around his backhand to take the ball on his forehand or against someone who attacks your serve and comes in, hit a slice serve, because the ball will move away from him.

Fig. 54. At point of contact *on the serve, two parts of the body should be in a straight line—the* left *leg and* right *arm.*

Fig. 55. A major limitation of the two-handed backhand is the limited reach on wide balls, especially when returning serve on a wide topspin or "twist" serve when you may not have time to take the extra steps necessary to get to the ball.

This presumes that you can hit a slice, topspin, and flat serve. If you can't, your game is limited to what you can do. My strong recommendation is that you begin immediately to develop all three serves. Go out and practice until you can hit these serves and then test them in match play. If you don't, you'll definitely be limited.

2. CHECKPOINTS FOR THE SERVE

Think "Wrist" on the Serve

Most pros teach that the toss is the most important part of the serve. They have their students practice tossing the ball so that it will land in a chalked-out area just in front of them or do some other drill to "groove" the perfect toss. This is nonsense, because there are four times when the perfect toss won't be possible:

1. On a windy day if you toss to your regular height the ball will blow off course. The toss, therefore, must be lower.
2. When the sun is in your favorite toss spot you must alter the toss to one side or the other to avoid blinding yourself.
3. When you're nervous—it's match point against you or you're playing mixed doubles and you've just served two double faults in a row and your partner is wondering whether you'll *ever* get it in—jumpy nerves will alter your toss.
4. The tossing hand is often uncoordinated. If you're right-handed and you throw a ball left-handed, you know how ridiculous you can look. The toss is just as difficult a chore for the left hand to perform, and, therefore, you probably won't always get a dependable toss.

Instead of the toss, concentrate on the wrist. The wrist is critical because it causes the serve to go wherever it goes—left, right, long or short. Hitting the ball short or long is related to the snapping up or down of the wrist. Hitting it left or right is caused by rotating the wrist to the left or right. If the ball is going into the net, think "hit up." If the ball is going long, think "snap down." To help your wrist remain strong enough to do what you want it to, give it a rest before the serve (see Fig. 56).

Fig. 56. Relax the serving hand prior to starting the service motion. This will help to maintain a loose wrist throughout the serve.

Chapter Eleven
Simplicity Checkpoints
for the Dropshot and
Counter-dropshot

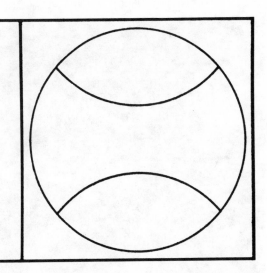

1. HITTING THE DROPSHOT

The main thing to remember on a dropshot is that the ball should have a good "arc." Many players mistakenly believe a dropshot should be hit flat (without an arc) so it gets there faster and thus gives the opponent less time to get to the ball. In the first place, the dropshot is not a winner. It is a *setup* shot. You should have in mind that your opponent will get to the ball just before the second bounce, which means he will be close to the net and be forced to hit the ball up. That enables you to volley his return more easily if you move into the net and to pass more easily from the baseline. On a successful dropshot, then, the first and second bounces should be as close together as possible. A good dropshot bounces at least twice, and preferably three times, inside the service box. Therefore, all dropshots are hit with backspin, because backspin "pulls" the ball toward the first bounce. Manuel Santana had so much backspin on his dropshots that he could often make it hop back over to his side of the net for an outright winner. Backspin also keeps the ball low, which forces your opponent to contact the ball below the level of the net. If he takes the ball above the net and he's at the net, he's in the double offensive position, which means he'll probably end the point on that shot.

You don't *need* much backswing for a dropshot, but if you always take a short backswing your opponent will know what's coming (see Fig. 57).

The proper way to hit a dropshot is to first make contact behind the ball and then rotate the wrist under so the strings *point* to the sky. The more the wrist is rotated, so that the strings turn under the ball, the greater will be the backspin. The racquet ends at the level you contact the ball (usually waist level) with the racquet face open. Keep the wrist firm but flexible, and the arm bent (see Fig. 58). A dropshot is a delicate shot, and the "feel" or "touch" it takes to properly execute a dropshot *cannot* be taught. It comes, first of all, through the understanding of contact area. And there will be many days (even after you understand contact area) when you won't have the proper touch because of high winds or a fast court or because your opponent hits with so much spin or pace that your touch vanishes.

Fig. 57. Often a player will give away his dropshot by using very little backswing on a dropshot and a much longer backswing on a ground stroke.

Fig. 58. On a dropshot, the arm must be bent on contact. A player who hits his forehand with a straight arm can seldom hit an accurate, reliable dropshot.

2. FIVE TIMES YOU SELDOM HIT A DROPSHOT

Basically, there are five times when you seldom hit a dropshot:

1. Against a hard-hit ball
2. When the wind is at your back
3. On a fast surface
4. Against a high-bouncing ball
5. When you're behind the baseline

When the ball is hit hard, or when you're playing on a fast surface, it is much more difficult to feel the ball and therefore more difficult to dropshot. Also on a fast surface, or when the wind is at your back, the ball tends to skid toward your opponent, making the all-important second bounce land too deep. When the ball is bouncing high above your shoulder or when you're behind the baseline your shot must travel a long distance in the air, thus giving your opponent plenty of time to take the ball above the white band and put it away.

Also, if you know the five basic times when you seldom dropshot, you can prevent your opponent from wearing you out with dropshots. Hit deep, which will give you plenty of time to get to his dropshots, or add more pace, which will hinder your opponent's feel.

3. THE COUNTER-DROPSHOT

The answer when your opponent hits a good dropshot is to counter-dropshot or hit deep down the line. To successfully counter-dropshot you must be able to hit the dropshot and the deep down-the-line shot with the same preparation. In other words, you must be able to *disguise* both shots. Your racquet preparation should be the same for both shots. But for the deep shot you simply lengthen the contact area, and for a dropshot you turn under the ball.

4. CHECKPOINTS FOR THE DROPSHOT

The checkpoints for the dropshot are relatively simple:

1. Finish with the strings pointing up to the sky and the racquet face parallel to the ground.
2. Make the ball bounce at least twice inside the service box and preferably three or four times.

Chapter Twelve
Simplicity Checkpoints for the Lob and the Overhead

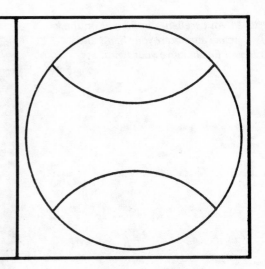

1. LOBBING IS SMART

Players who lob are intelligent players. The lob is not just a desperation shot when all else fails or a shot only girls try. The lob is both a setup shot and an offensive weapon. For example, it is the only shot you should hit when a player crowds the net, because he's cut off most of your angles and avenues for a passing shot, and he's in too close to successfully cover even a mediocre lob. Also, it's often a good idea to lob frequently in the beginning of the match just to see if your opponent can even hit an overhead and to show him you know how to lob. If you never lob, the opponent can crowd the net, and if he does this you'll never be able to hit a passing shot either. The player who never lobs, therefore, is one of the easiest players to beat.

2. CHECKPOINTS FOR THE LOB

The Hand and Racquet Finish Above Your Head

How high you follow through depends on several variables—the wind, the height of your opponent, and whether you're hitting an offensive or defensive lob—but both the hand and the racquet should finish above your head (see Fig. 59). Outdoors, if the wind is at your back the apex should be closer to you, and if you're hitting into the wind the apex should be farther back on the other side of the net. Against a very tall opponent, make sure you aim higher, which means finishing higher. And, finally, an offensive lob should get quickly over the opponent's reach, so it's hit with a lower arc than a defensive lob.

Remember, a lob is a ground stroke, and all the principles of a ground stroke apply, including the use of the left hand to open and close the racquet face for more or less height, contact area to add depth, and balance.

Fig. 59. An excellent checkpoint on the lob is to make sure both your hand and racquet finish above your head.

3. CHECKPOINTS FOR THE OVERHEAD

Set Up Quickly for the Overhead

The elbow of the racquet arm should be up when preparing to hit an overhead. The racquet head can be anywhere, but if your elbow is pointing to the sky you will always be ready to swing.

Since the ball is rapidly gaining speed as it falls, it is difficult to judge when the ball is at the proper height to swing. So, the left hand should point at the ball as a guide to help your depth perception.

Stand sideways to the ball. Trying to hit an overhead while facing the net is as difficult to do as facing the net while serving. Without the proper shoulder turn you lose most of your potential for power. Remember, it's called the overhead "smash," not the overhead "poop." Hit it with the intention of putting the ball away.

To test your preparation, try the exercise shown in Fig. 60.

Reach Up, Snap Down

Once you are properly prepared (see Fig. 61), remind yourself to reach up and snap down (see Fig. 62). Most overhead errors arise because the player swings after the ball has dropped too low (because the player misjudges the rapidly accelerating ball), which causes the ball to land in the net. Or hitting too long, because he did not snap his wrist downward while contacting the ball, which causes the ball to be hit long. A stiff, locked wrist inevitably causes a long hit and is usually caused by lack of confidence.

4. FOUR TIMES YOU LET THE BALL BOUNCE ON AN OVERHEAD

There are four basic times when you should let the ball bounce before you hit an overhead:

1. When the ball is lobbed very high
2. When the ball is lobbed very deep
3. When it's very windy
4. When the sun is in your eyes

The overhead is the one stroke in which there isn't much room for adjustment once you start to swing. So, when the ball has the potential to go off course (in a stiff wind) or is very difficult to judge (when the ball is lobbed very high or deep or the sun is in your eyes), let the ball bounce, step up, and smash it away.

5. DRILLS FOR THE OVERHEAD

The four-square drill

Once you have a pretty decent overhead, divide the court into four squares and see if you can hit all four.

The hot-box drill

Get a few friends and position one man at the baseline, one or two players at the IVP, and one player on the other side hitting overheads. The player at the baseline tries to lob the overheads back, and the players at the net work on "reaction volleys." You can see where this drill got its name.

Fig. 60. Here's an exercise for overhead preparation. Have someone hit a lob to you, but instead of hitting the ball, catch it in your left hand and freeze. Check for three things: (1) Are your left hand and arm up? (2) Is your right arm in the "scratch the back" position? (3) Are you turned sideways?

Fig. 61. When you're actually hitting the overhead, it should look as if you're planning to catch the ball in your left hand, just as you did in the previous exercise (Fig. 60).

Fig. 62. Then reach up and snap down! Remember the overhead is a smash, not an overhead poop.

*Phase Four
Understanding
Strategy*

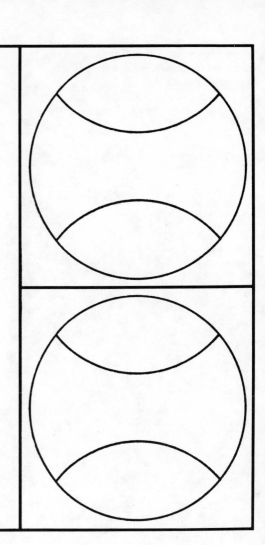

Chapter Thirteen
Pre-match Strategy

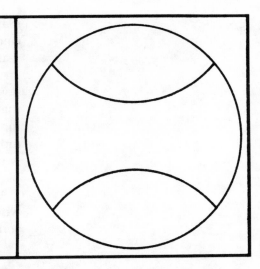

1. WHAT IS STRATEGY?

Most players think of strategy as some secret grandiose plan that only the top pros with their great instinct for the game could ever devise. Tennis *is* complex strategically, but most of that strategy is thought out well in advance. It concerns different surfaces, different climatic conditions, the weaknesses of the opponent, and many other factors. Very little strategy involves outthinking your opponent right in the heat of battle. In fact, you can easily overwork strategy and the need for it. Players become so entangled in the mental part of the game they end up tripping over their minds on the way over to hit the ball.

Understanding the game is the key to effective strategy. Strategy is not something you just tack onto the rest of your game. It is an integral part of understanding tennis and is inseparable from the rest of the game. If your strategy is weak, the first step is to reread Phase One, "Understanding the Game," because if you understand the game your strategy will automatically be a lot better.

Many players have an idea of strategy as "I'm gonna hit the ball here, then there, then over there." But it doesn't work that way. You must distinguish between strategy and instinct. We watch the top players move the ball around and pull off a brilliant sequence of shots. But let me assure you, most of those shots are instinct. They feel where the ball should go by thousands of hours of match play.

2. HAVE A PLAN

Many players show up at the court with no idea at all how they will play their opponent. How many times have you heard someone say after he's already played a set and a half, "Oh, you're a left-hander. That's the problem!" Most players are unaware of the most obvious things. The most important strategy whether you're a beginner or a touring pro is that you *have* a strategy.

A football team prepares all week for a game. They study the opposing team and work out every detail of their game plan. But in tennis it's amazing how many players arrive at the court without the vaguest notion of what their strategy will be that day. The most effective strategy is made before the match begins, because there's not much time for thinking during a point. Once you're under pressure there's not much real strategy, it's mostly reactions.

At most levels, most of the time, the most important strategy is preparation—knowing what you're going to do according to the elements involved that day (Are you playing on a clay or hard court? At sea level or in the mountains? At high noon or under lights? During a small hurricane or indoors?) and knowing who your opponent is (Does he play left-handed or two-handed? Is he a ground-stroker or volleyer? Is he a hard hitter or a touch player?).

A good strategist is a player who has an overall understanding of the game, who can formulate an effective game plan, and then, when all else fails, has some alternative recourse.

3. SCOUT YOUR OPPONENT

Be certain, especially in a tournament, that you know well in advance whom you're playing. And if you're serious about winning, if you get mad when you lose, if you destroy your spouse's life for two days after a bad loss, then it's worth the time and effort to scout your opponent.

Many players, for some reason, think of scouting as if it were spying on the opponent (almost cheating), but scouting is a much-practiced and highly useful method of increasing your understanding of the game. I'm not suggesting that you follow your opponent to his private court and spy on him with binoculars. But why not sit down and closely study a player at your club whom you have trouble beating or whom you know you're going to play next week in the club championship? Heck, he'd probably be flattered.

On the circuit the scrutinizing of other players is a constant pastime. I remember once sitting with Pancho Gonzales while watching Rod Laver play in the late 60's at the Canadian Open. Gonzales told me, "Watch Laver's right hip on his serve. When he stops turning his right hip completely, that's when he's tired." Because Laver was not a strong server he tended to tire toward the end of a match on his serve. Pancho said, "Watch that!"—and sure enough, Laver's hip stayed open and he started serving shorter and then a couple double faults crept in. And he almost lost the match. Of course, that's a very subtle perception. But often the most obvious observations can be the most effective in developing a good strategy.

I played Jean Francois Caujolle in 1975 on a fast Laykold court the day after he'd come from playing on the grass at Wimbledon. Francois was a much better player than I was. (He beat Jimmy Connors in 1980.) I hadn't played circuit tennis for two years, and he was highly ranked in the world. I was clearly outclassed.

There was hope, though. I figured that Francois had only that morning to adjust to the courts, so I wrote down all the things he'd have trouble adjusting to—all the differences between grass and hard courts. For example, the ball stays very low on grass and the footing is precarious compared to hard courts. So I basically did two things. I lofted the ball high and rushed the net, and with the ball up around his shoulders (a ball he hadn't handled in over a month), his returns floated back and I was able to put them away. Also, having been on the bad footing of grass he was accustomed to taking his first volley later, usually behind the service line. On a hard court you can gamble and often get two or three feet inside the service line and still change direction effectively. But on grass if you gamble like that you may slip and be flat on your face. So I stepped in on his service and made him play all my returns early. And here was a guy who without a doubt was twice as good a player as I was, and simply by adjusting two parts of my game I was able to win the match 6–2, 6–2. And the only reason I won was that I took the time to analyze my opponent.

4. TAKING NOTES

Closely related to scouting is note-taking. Tennis is a complex game, because every opponent is different, every court is different, every time of day presents different problems. There are so many variables in tennis that it becomes impossible for the mind to juggle all this information and come up with the right piece of information at the right time unless you have some written system for remembering.

Carry a little notebook in your tennis bag, or if you plan to someday play extensive tournament tennis use index cards you can shuffle and file. But no matter how you take your notes, you'll begin to notice patterns developing, things you do over and over again. These are usually your weaknesses, and simply by jotting down your problems you can begin to see where you need to improve. This one technique alone, notetaking, without extra practice or getting in shape or buying a new rocket-powered racquet, will make you a better tennis player, because it will help you understand your game better.

Basically, you should take notes on two types of information:

1. General tennis knowledge. Why do volleys have backspin? How do you vary depth or length or spin? Why and when should you hit a dropshot?
2. Personal observations. How do you react in different match situations? How do your opponents react?

5. WARM-UP

Contrary to how most club players treat the warm-up, it is not the time to practice your strokes. If you don't have the strokes when you arrive for the match, a fifteen-minute warm-up won't improve them. The warm-up should be a period of *observation* of your opponent, not a time to get your game together. So don't focus your attention on yourself but rather on your opponent.

Try to start the warm-up at the net, because it's a perfect place to analyze the other player. He will usually go through his entire repertoire of shots while you volley. Give him different speeds and different spins to see how he handles them. If his lead heel (the left heel on a forehand, the right heel on a backhand) is planted, it usually means he has confidence in that side. The farther over he steps (the more closed his stance), the more prone he is to go down the line; the more open he stands, the more prone he is to go crosscourt. If he always takes his racquet back open on the backhand, he'll probably float his backhand passing shot under pressure, particularly if the approach is hit without much pace. If he hits with a Continental grip, he's vulnerable to high balls on the forehand.

You can also use different strategies in the warm-up. You can play totally to your opponent's strength or totally to his weakness. If you play his strength he'll gain confidence in the warm-up, but as soon as you go to his weakness in the match it may fall apart because it's not warm. Or, if you go to his weakness in the warm-up and then play his strength immediately in the match, his strength will sometimes break down. (An important point, of course, is to warm up all your *own* strokes.) Also, if a player needs a lot of rhythm, don't give him any in the warm-up. Hit the ball as hard as you can. Then, when the game starts, give him nothing but "puff" balls, chips, and dinks.

Finally, play well in the warm-up. It can be a big psychological advantage—often a match is over midway through the warm-up. That's why I've always gone out and hit for an hour or so right up until I have to play. Have the groove, be physically and mentally sharp in warm-up. Make very few mistakes and you'll put a lot of pressure on your opponent.

Chapter Fourteen
Match Strategy, Part I:
Strengths and Weaknesses

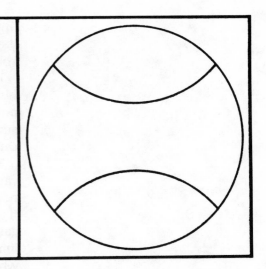

Your strategy can be effective only if you're in the match, only if you're not hopelessly outclassed. And you can be in a match in which you lose the first eleven games. If you're playing someone better than you, make sure you play your game. Try to make the opponent go your way. The first two or three games are critical. Decide your game plan and try to make it work. Often a person playing a tough opponent will lose the first couple of games and then he'll panic and try to hit hard with an opponent who can clearly outgun him.

Don't try to do what you're not capable of doing. In other words, don't use a strategy you can't execute. The basic premise of good strategy, then, is to know your limitations. So many times you'll see a player take a shot he has no business trying. Tactics are useless unless you are capable of hitting the shots. Therefore, you must develop an awareness of what you can do and then be realistic about it. Players often have aspirations to attain a level that is totally unrealistic, and as a result they experience a lot of frustration. And when you're frustrated you're not progressing.

It's important to understand that your limitations and capabilities change from day to day. Some days you've got all your weapons, some days you don't. There are mornings when you bounce out of bed and mornings when it is absolute agony to get up. Or what if you just got a traffic ticket before you got to the court or you had a fight with your wife or you lost your life savings because gold went back down to $35 an ounce? I can't recall playing even five matches when everything was perfect—perfect weather, perfect crowd, *and* I felt good. About 99.9 percent of the time that I've stepped on the court, *something* was wrong.

The player who thinks he can win only when he's got all his weapons, only when he's playing his best, will almost never win. Often a player will go out on the court and if he can't hit all his strokes that day the match is over. He can't win. He judges his game by his best day and tries to live up to that standard, which is unrealistic. Those perfect days when you're in the "zone" come about once a year.

There are also players who insist on playing as if they *do* have all their weapons every day. They also seldom win. You've got to play according to your limitations, and those limitations change every day from morning to afternoon—every match, every set, every game. How often have you seen a player's serve desert him after he's just served the last game at love? Or double-fault the next serve after an ace? Not only do you play a different opponent in tennis but your game is almost never the same—you are never the same player. You may hear a pro say, "You got it!"—but no one's "got it." You may have it today but it'll be gone tomorrow.

It takes an extremely intelligent and mature person to get the most out of his game at every moment. If you're not executing your normal shots, you must have the intelligence and courage to change your game and adjust your strategy. You know you're a good player when your games fall apart and you can still win the match.

There are two basic guidelines for assessing your limitations and capabilities. First, match assessment. If you try to maneuver a guy around the court and you just can't get your dropshot to clear the net, that's a limitation. If you're tired, don't try to bomb aces. If you have a leg injury, avoid a running game. Second, practice sessions are the time to assess your general overall limitations and capabilities. In other words, in practice try to understand where your game is generally. Know, for example, before you go out for a match that you can't hit a topspin backhand passing shot down the line, so don't try it.

Specific areas for assessment of your limitations and capabilities include:

1. How mobile are you? Do you have the ability to change direction easily? Are your reactions quick? How is your overall foot speed?
2. Can you hit the ball in any direction—crosscourt and down the line?
3. How well can you hit spins (backspin, topspin, and sidespin)?
4. How fully have you mastered placements? Can you hit the seven target zones?

1. LIKES AND DISLIKES

Everyone has his likes and dislikes on the tennis court—his favorite shot, one position he's most comfortable in, the speed he likes to hit the ball. There isn't a player in the world who likes to serve and volley and ground-stroke equally well. Everyone has a preference.

In every other sport the opponent gives you what you don't like. A pitcher will find out what the batter likes, and he rarely lets him see that pitch. A defense in football will find out what the opposing quarterback and halfback like to do, and then set up to take away that strength. In almost every sport the goal is to take away the opponent's strength, but in tennis it's rarely taught.

You can tell what a player likes to do by the shots he always takes. It's that easy. For example, most women players around the country at the C and B levels stand at the baseline and bang balls at each other. No dropshots. No angles. Nothing but hitting the ball back. They seldom come to the net—even in warm-up—so you can be absolutely sure they hate to volley. Another typical situation is the guy who never takes overheads in warm-up. He may pretend that his overhead is so devastating he doesn't need to warm it up, but you can bet it's because he doesn't have one.

As soon as you've determined what your opponent doesn't like, proceed to make him unhappy.

2. THE THREE E'S—EMERGENCY, EXPLOITATION, AND EXECUTION

There isn't a player in the world who is free from weaknesses—even Bjorn Borg. There are many things a player can or cannot do. But determining strengths and weaknesses can become very complex. For example, a player's forehand volley may be strong on high balls but weak on low balls. The key to determining an opponent's weaknesses is through the understanding of exploitation.

The whole concept of effective strategy is based on the triple-E theory—emergency, exploitation, and execution. If you're on defense, you should think "emergency." If you're on offense, you should think "exploitation" in order to put your opponent in an emergency. Force your opponent to hit shots he cannot or does not like to handle and he'll feel pressure. And the pressure will cause a breakdown—an emergency. If you handle emergencies effectively, exploit your opponent at every opportunity, and "execute" your shots well, you will be very hard to beat that day.

The Two Opposites

Most players think "attack" means hitting harder and running faster. But attack is the exploitation of an opponent's weaknesses. And the greatest tool for exploiting your opponent is the utilization of *the two opposites.* There are two opposites to every facet of tennis. Find the one with which your opponent has trouble. Forehand or backhand? High shots or low? Hard or soft? Shots hit wide or right at him? Making him run for every ball or giving him all day to hit a shot? Divide the court into baseline and net play—does he serve and volley or ground-stroke better? Then divide the court into deuce and ad court—is he stronger on the backhand or the forehand? Then check his movement—does he move better laterally or up and back? In other words, pick his game apart. Every player has areas of weakness and strength and preference. I guarantee you that no player will do all things well.

To exploit your opponent, however, you must develop capabilities to exploit him, which means understanding how a ball bounces. If you want to hit a ball low you must understand how to hit it and what will happen after you hit it. The majority of players cannot progress, cannot beat better players, because they don't understand how to exploit their opponent.

A player's strengths depend mostly on whom he's playing that day. A strength against one opponent is a weakness against another. What usually works against some players may not work against others. The circumstances change with the opponent. If a player can't hit a low volley, it usually takes a pretty good opponent to make him play his volleys low. Against a weak player you can avoid situations in which you are vulnerable.

Often a player doesn't realize when he's being exploited. He usually thinks he's just not hitting well that day. "Geez! My backhand was horrible today!" But his backhand probably was no better or worse than any other day. He just ran into an opponent who understood how to exploit his game.

3. COMMON WEAKNESSES

There are several common weaknesses that, like disease, know no class distinctions. That is, they afflict the king of the courts all the way down to the bottom player on the C ladder, from the top tournament player to the raw beginner.

Overconfidence and Lack of Confidence

One day at a tournament in Hawaii, while waiting for my first-round match to start, I sat next to a young fellow who was telling everyone that he was sure to win this tournament because where he came from they played "real tennis." So somebody asked him who his first-round opponent was and he replied, "Some guy named Burwash." He went on long enough to get me steamed, so I won all 48 points in our match to win 6–0, 6–0. Afterward he came up to me and said, "I learned a real good lesson today. To keep my mouth shut!"

Don't ever start thinking that your opponent is a good or a bad player, because you're setting yourself up for defeat through overconfidence or lack of confidence. A good player may play badly or a poor player may play out of his head that day. A player will often lose a match because he arrives at the court thinking, "Geez, I don't even have to warm up today, this guy's so bad." Then he goes out on the court and starts toying around, and before he knows it he's behind. Instead, always assume your opponent will never make a mistake. If he does make a mistake, that's a bonus. That's what made Ken Rosewall so great—he knew that on any given day he could be beaten. As a result, overconfidence rarely crept in and he seldom lost to an inferior player.

Lack of Consistency

Consistency is closely related to rhythm, and usually if you can break up a player's rhythm you can break up his consistency. Never allow the opponent to remain in the area he likes if you want to break up his consistency. There isn't a player in the world who is consistent from everywhere on the court.

If you're playing someone who seems steady, remember the "two opposites." There's a high and a low, a hard and a soft, a topspin and a backspin. The player who is a "steady" player usually likes to do only one thing. He will stay on the baseline or serve and volley. Very seldom does he do both consistently—even Borg has a preference.

Players Who Can't Handle Pressure

Some players have great-looking strokes but they can't hold up under either physical or mental pressure. A player who can't handle physical pressure is easy to spot. Any kind of full-out aggressive attack will force him to commit errors. Or he'll hit a weak shot, the ball will come back defensively, and you can easily put it away.

Those players who cannot stand up to the mental pressures of a match are more difficult to spot. Watch your opponent closely at the changeover when he's toweling off. His hand may be shaking or he may do something else that betrays his nervousness. The serve, however, is usually the best tip-off of jangled nerves. If your opponent begins to miss the serve by a lot or he starts double-faulting or his arm starts shaking in the ready position or his toss goes way off the mark, it's usually a sign that he's feeling the pressure. That's the time to attack with even more determination.

Poor Conditioning

There are players who are very good ground-strokers. They can bang winners from anywhere on the court and love pressure—the tighter the match the more accurate they become. But they may be out of shape. A player like that will often win by scores like 6-0, 7-5. He always annihilates his opponent in the first set and almost never wins a three-setter. In other words, his strokes and his effectiveness diminish as the match goes on. This is not uncommon. In fact, nearly everyone's strokes worsen with fatigue. It's natural. As the body tires, nerves and muscles and major organs don't function as well. A player who bombs aces in the first two or three games may not be able to keep it up for two or three sets. That's what makes Roscoe Tanner's serve so great. It's not the fastest ever (though it's very nearly the fastest) but he can still blast it 120 mph in the fifth set. Not many other players today can do that.

If you know or suspect an opponent is out of shape (his lack of mobility or a prodigious beer gut are pretty good indications), then run him for three or four games and see how he holds up. He may win the first four games and then fold and never hit another decent shot all day.

Bobby Riggs, winner of the over-60s grand slam (the national grass, clay, hard, and indoor championships) told me that when he plays a match on the senior circuit he doesn't care who wins the first set. His only thought is to wear down his opponent. A typical Riggs score is 4-6, 6-2, 6-0. When you're playing an opponent who's through for the day and there are still two sets to go, the match is yours.

If you suspect an opponent is out of shape, test him. If he fails the test he will probably never beat you again—until he shapes up.

4. BUSTING STRENGTHS

Most strategy involves finding an opponent's strength and then denying him the chance to use it. The only exception is when you decide to "bust" your opponent's strength. The basic theory in busting a strength is to put so much pressure on your opponent's strength that the strength folds and then his confidence folds and with that his entire game crumbles.

There's more to busting a strength than simply pounding the ball at your opponent's forehand. The key is the utilization of the "two opposites." If a player has a big forehand he usually has a big forehand in a certain way. He either hits it flat or with topspin or he's got great direction or great pace or disguise. Very few players have a strength that is strong in every way.

If your opponent has a great forehand, start with backspins, then throw him topspin, make him run, or float the ball at him. See if he can handle them all. Also, a player with a strong shot usually has rhythm, so give him dropshots, side-T placements, and chip shots. If you get him out of his groove he may begin to suspect his "weapon" isn't all that potent.

Some players' greatest weapon is their legs. Against a runner, hit the ball back to the spot where he just came from, because a player who depends on his speed will usually try to leave ahead of time. He'll break for the open court before you hit the ball, which, of course, leaves the court open where he just came from.

Another way to counter a runner is to hit down the center, because a runner will usually hit the ball better on the run. He's running so much he doesn't know what it's like to hit standing still. Again, give the opponent what he doesn't like.

Remember, just as your own game changes from day to day, so does your opponent's. Look for signs that his strength is not quite as strong that day.

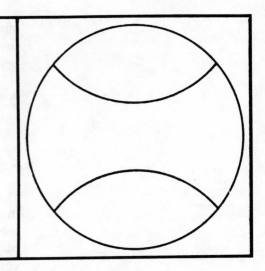

Chapter Fifteen
Match Strategy, Part II: Match Situations

1. PRIORITIES VERSUS PERCENTAGES

I don't stress percentages because I don't really think people understand percentages. In fact, a great percentage of the time percentages do not make sense. For example, if the percentage suggests a down-the-line approach to the opponent's backhand and the opponent has the greatest backhand since Don Budge, is that a high-percentage shot?

There are books that plot out exactly the percentage of times you should hit your serves, ground strokes, and volleys to a certain spot. But that approach is extremely misleading, because percentages change according to the circumstances, whom your opponent is, and where and when the match is played. Where and when you hit each shot is determined much more by priorities than percentages.

Priorities take precedence over percentages, and your priority is to go to the opponent's vulnerabilities, to the opponent's weaknesses. If your opponent doesn't have any vulnerabilities you can exploit over and over, you play the percentages. If you can't exploit your opponent through priorities or percentages, you've got a match on your hands.

Your overall game plan is determined by priorities. For example, if your opponent has a weak backhand, your priority is to exploit the backhand. Every time you play, you play someone different, you have a different game plan—so the percentages change with the situation. What may be a high-percentage shot against one player is suicide against another. According to classical percentage strategy, for example, you should serve to the backhand 70 to 80 percent of the time, but if your opponent can't return your slice serve to the deuce court, then, of course, you should slice a lot to his forehand.

You always have two or three possibilities in a match. And the success of a good tennis player depends on his ability to select and place those possibilities in their correct priorities. For example, if you're playing an opponent who is very vulnerable on one side, but it's a very swirling, windy day, you can no longer think about playing to his weakness. Your priority is trying to figure out which direction the wind is blowing and how you can get the ball back somewhere in the court. On a very hot day your priority may be different than on a cool day. Instead of serving and volleying you may want to save your energy and try to make your opponent run.

Your own strengths can be your priorities. Forget the opponent if your strength is stronger than his strength. You don't have to worry about percentages at all. Like Eddie Dibbs and Harold Solomon, your priority becomes to run around your backhand and crack your forehand every time. If, on the other hand, your weakness is weaker than your opponent's weakness, your priority becomes to protect your weakness.

2. THE RETURN OF SERVE

There is one situation in tennis when percentages become your priority—on the return of serve. When returning serve you should have some preconceived idea of what you want to do with the ball. For instance, if you're playing a serve-and-volleyer you should hit low backspin returns to his feet. If you're playing a baseliner you should aim for good clearance of the net and good depth.

Percentages concerning the return of serve are fairly rigid and are based entirely on where the serve is hit.

On a Serve to the Forehand in the Forehand Court

If it's a hard serve, you should hit 80 percent of your returns crosscourt. This involves the principle that you should seldom change the direction of a hard-hit ball. This is based on the "angle of incidence equals the angle of reflection" phenomenon in physics—if a ray of light hits a perfectly flat surface, the ray will reflect off at exactly the same angle. In tennis terms, if you hit the ball back crosscourt where it came from, there is a great deal of room for error even on a fast serve. But if you try to change the ball's direction by going down the line, your timing and the angle of the racquet face must be exact. That's why when a player tries to go down the line in those circumstances the ball often goes way wide. If the serve is soft you can hit 80 percent of your returns down the line to the backhand, but whenever you're in trouble the best shot is crosscourt.

On a Serve to the Backhand in the Forehand Court

Regardless of the speed of the serve, return 80 percent down the line. One of the most difficult shots in tennis is trying to return crosscourt off the backhand in the deuce court.

On a Serve to the Forehand in the Backhand Court

If the ball is hit hard, the best percentage is to go down the center. Or if you're really accurate, try to hit to the backhand side. If it's a soft ball, pound it 80 percent to the opponent's backhand.

On a Serve to the Backhand in the Backhand Court

Return 80 percent crosscourt. If the server tries to make it all the way to the net (by not check-stepping at the service line), lob.

Following percentages on the return of serve will get you the best results.

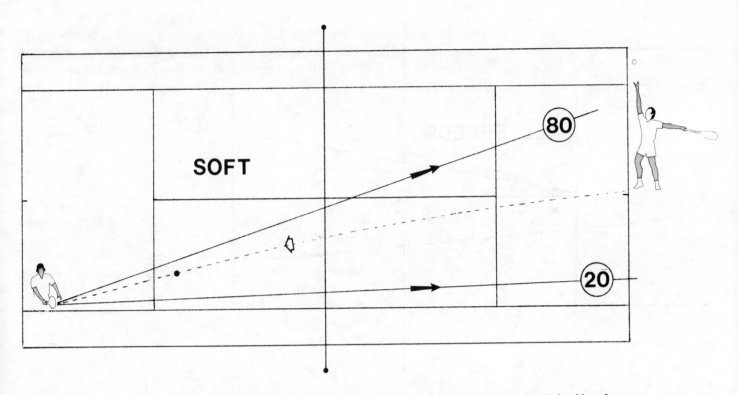

Diagram 5a. On a soft serve to your forehand in the deuce court, hit 80 percent deep to your opponent's backhand.

Diagram 5b. On a hard serve to your forehand in the deuce court, return the ball crosscourt. This is based on the principle that you should seldom change the direction of a hard-hit ball.

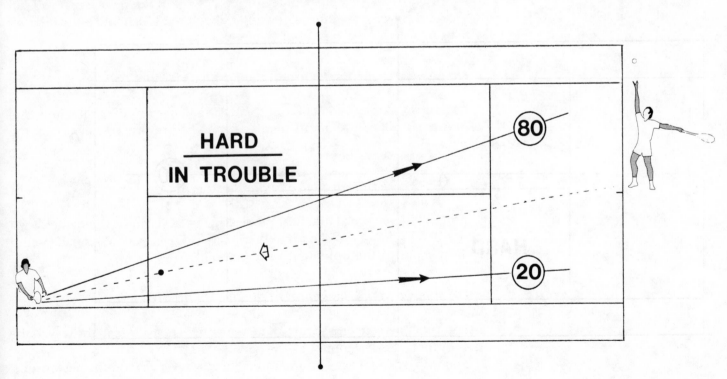

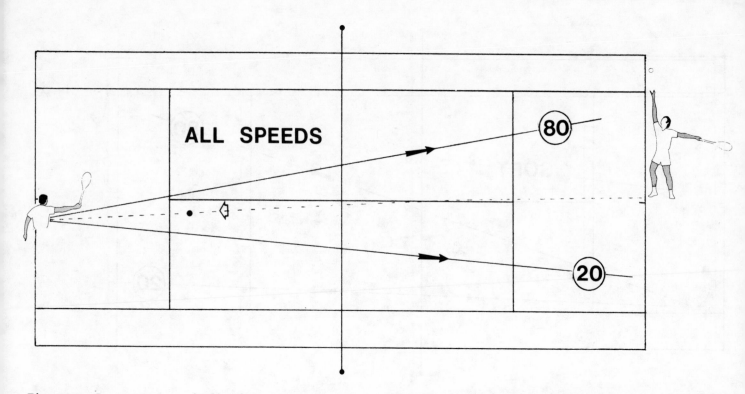

Diagram 5c. *On a serve to your backhand, your percentage return on all speeds is 80 percent to your opponent's backhand side. This neutralizes the return.*

Diagram 5d. *In the ad court, on a hard serve to the forehand side, the best return is down the center.*

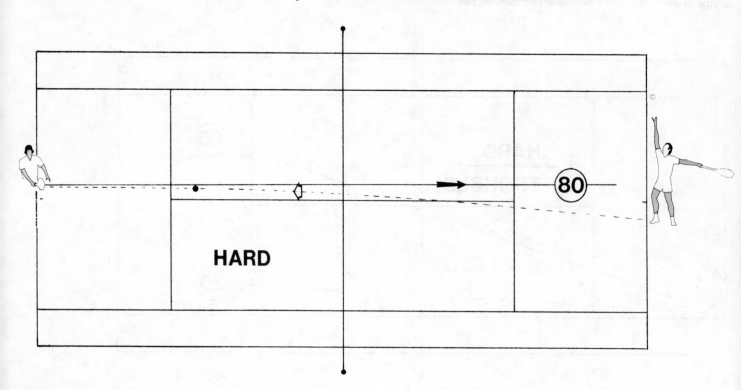

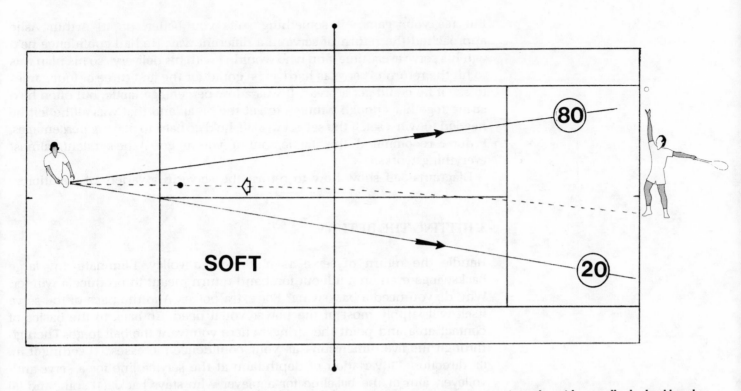

Diagram 5e. On a soft serve to the forehand in the ad court, hit 80 percent to your opponent's weaker side, usually the backhand.

Diagram 5f. On all backhand returns in the ad court, return 80 percent crosscourt.

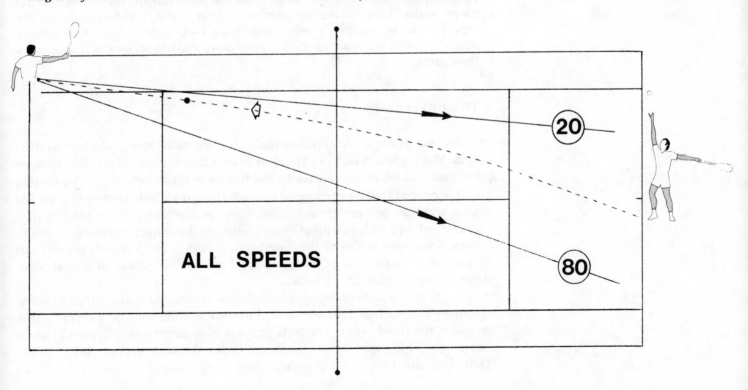

But it's your game—if something suits you better, do it! Arthur Ashe approached the return of serve in a different way. He had confidence he'd win his serve every time (and who wouldn't with his delivery), so his plan was to hit the return of serve as hard as he could for the first three or four games to see if he could get a break. It was a low-percentage tactic, but often he'd string together enough winners to get the break and that was all he felt he needed to win a set. If the set got to 4-all, he'd go back to playing percentages. I don't recommend this tactic, but if you've got Ashe's talent, almost everything works.

Diagrams 5a-f show how to return the serve in a variety of situations.

3. HITTING THE RETURN

Handle the return of serve as if it were a volley. Eliminate any large backswings even on a full-out forehand return meant to produce a winner. Why do you need a backswing? For extra power. And the pace of the serve itself will supply most of the power you'll need. Go back to the basics of contact area and point the strings where you want the ball to go. Then go through the five dimensions as your confidence increases: (1) getting it in, (2) direction, (3) variation of depth (aim at the service line for a serve-and-volleyer, aim at the baseline for a player who stays back), (4) spin, and (5) speed.

Wait for the return of serve with a forehand grip. If you don't have time to change to a backhand grip the forehand grip still allows you to hit a solid backspin backhand return. Using a backhand grip to hit a forehand return is just too awkward.

Three-man drill for the return of serve

The best drill for the return of serve is to have two players serving and volleying alternately to the returner. Play the point out and then have the next player serve. This eliminates the number-one problem when *practicing* the return of serve against a serve-and-volleyer—boredom. With two servers bombing away at a returner, he's always busy and the servers don't overwork their arms.

4. THE BIG POINTS

In every match there are certain points that are more important to win than others. The biggest point, of course, is match point. If you never win a match point you will never win a match. But there are other big points in a match, and it is crucial to the outcome of a match that you know what points are big points and that you are always particularly aware when you're playing one.

The third and fifth points of every game are the most important points in tennis. If you win both the third and fifth points of every game you will win aproximately 80 percent of your games. That's a fact—based on statistics I've done of match play at all levels.

There is an overwhelming psychological and strategical advantage to being ahead 40–love rather than 30–15, and that's the difference between winning or losing the third point. The fifth point is even more crucial. A 30–all game can go to game point for you at 40–30 or break point against you at 30–40. That, in a nutshell, is all the difference in the world.

40–30 is also a big point, because you can end the game on this point. I recommend serving and volleying at 40–30 regardless of the surface. Put the pressure in your opponent's corner and see how he handles it.

The fifth and seventh games are the most important games to win. The psychological aspects of tennis are so significant that the edge gained by winning one important game can make a runaway of a close set. A close set at 4–2 becomes a runaway at 5–2 or a tooth-and-nail battle at 4–3. Other examples: 3–1 becomes 4–1 or 3–2; 4–0 becomes 4–1 or 5–0; 3–all becomes 4–3 or 3–4. Those are very crucial splits.

If you've been awake you've probably already figured out there are "super big points"—those points when big points and big games coincide. On the fifth point of the seventh game a circuit pro will run out of his shoes trying to win that point. Yet the club player who is totally unaware of the significance of the point may decide to try for a big backhand that hasn't a chance of going in.

When I was first on the pro circuit back in 1967, I played a very fine player from Mexico named Marcelo Lara. I had thirteen match points in the fifth set against him and I couldn't close out the match. I was a nobody on the circuit and he was ranked very high, so I was under intense pressure whenever I reached match point. And, under pressure, nearly everyone tends to play more conservatively. I'd get to my ad and I'd stay back on match point. I did it thirteen times in a row and Marcelo would get me in a rally (he was much better from the baseline than I was), and finally he won the match. That was an important lesson for me.

Put the pressure on your opponent on big points. It's a very rare human being who, when you put him under pressure, can counterpressure you. Particularly watch a player's strokes at key points. That's when you can most easily spot his weaknesses, because that's when he's most nervous and therefore most vulnerable to a breakdown. If he has a shaky forehand it will do most of its shaking on the big points.

5. POINT COMBINATIONS

A point combination is the combining together of two or more shots in such a way that one shot makes the following shot more effective. Often in a match you're either the one putting together a combination of shots or you're the one trying to dig out of it.

Point combinations are very important to good strategy, but they must be learned through experience. They depend so much on the opponent, the circumstances, and your ability to execute shots that I could diagram literally hundreds of possibilities and still not give you any greater understanding of the game. So I'll simply introduce a couple of the most commonly used and least complicated combinations and let you build from there.

The use of the side T's to open up the court and produce greater angles is, perhaps, the most common method for putting together an effective combination of shots. Once the court is open there are many places your next shot can be hit with telling effect.

Manuel Santana, the great clay-court player of the 1960's, who won nearly every tournament of significance, including Wimbledon and the U.S. Open, was perhaps the greatest practitioner of the "double side T." He would hit the ball with tremendous topspin from side T to side T. Before his opponent could get to the ball it would already be outside the doubles alley. So back and forth he'd go for fifteen to twenty shots until his legs got rubbery. And then Manuel would dropshot to the opposite corner for a winner. It was his favorite maneuver, and with it he won almost every tournament in the world of any significance.

Another classic point combination involves the "diagonal theory." There are only two diagonals on each side of the court—from a point at the net and one singles sideline to a point at the baseline and the far singles sideline. If you hit a dropshot to one point of the diagonal and the next shot to the far corner, you will force the opponent to run the most amount of steps to get to the ball.

The purpose of the diagonal theory is not necessarily to win the point but to wear out your opponent. It is also an excellent way to break up an opponent's rhythm, especially that of a good ground-stroker, because fatigue often brings on a lack of muscle coordination and inevitably destroys a player's rhythm.

My personal realization of how effective the diagonal theory can be came when I was playing at the Parklands Club in Nairobi, Kenya, in 1969, at a fairly high altitude. My opponent dropshotted me and lobbed me unmercifully for the first three games. I was so worn out and confused I thought to myself, "Geez! I don't know if I'll make it the entire set!" I figured if he could do this to me—and I don't tire easily—think of all those other players who would *really* be susceptible. And that's when I learned to open up the court.

6. THE D-N-O THEORY

A good golfer is usually hitting from a nice comfortable position in the middle of the fairway, while a beginner is usually in a trap or behind a tree. He's always out of position and he's constantly forced to make difficult shots. But where the beginner really runs into trouble is when he tries to reach the green through the trees. It's a career shot even for a pro, and the hacker wonders why it took him six shots to get out of the woods. A beginning tennis player is also usually out of position, so he, too, is usually hitting a difficult shot. But instead of trying to hit safe, the beginning tennis player, like the beginning golfer, usually tries a shot even McEnroe would be overjoyed to make.

This may sound a bit odd, but most players don't even know *when* they're in trouble, and that leads us to an explanation of the defense-neutral-offense theory, or D-N-O theory.

The D-N-O theory is based on two principles: (1) the ball in relationship to the white band that runs along the top of the net, and (2) the position of both players on the court.

The white band is really the divisional part of the defensive-offensive theory of playing. Once you contact the ball below the white band, you're in a defensive position. If you contact the ball above the white band, you're in an offensive position. Most players, therefore, make their errors when they try to make an offensive shot when the ball is below the white band.

Concerning the second principle, the position of both players on the court:

1. If both players are at the baseline, there's a neutral situation.
2. If both players are at the net, there's a neutral situation.
3. But if one player is at the net and one is at the baseline, there's an offensive-defensive situation.

So, for example, if a person is at the net (O) and he contacts the ball below the white band (D) he's neutralized (N). By the same token, if a player at the net (O) gets the ball above the white band he's in a double offensive position and the point will probably end on that shot.

Diagrams 6a-c show these situations.

Remember it's not the D-O-N theory; it's the D-N-O theory. Don't try to go from defense to offense on one shot. The key word is "neutralize." If you're in a defensive position with the other player at the net you have two ways to neutralize the opponent: you can either lob or make him volley from below the white band (see Figs. 63a-b).

To do the latter, hit a low chip shot or a quickly dipping topspin. This forces the opponent to hit a volley with an arc to it, which is not an offensive volley, and thus you've neutralized him. But most players think the only effective shot is to hit the ball past the net man. And considering the fact that tennis players even at the top levels are able to hit outright winners on only 5 to 10 percent of their passing shots, that's not smart tennis.

Now, in terms of the D-N-O theory, if you want to neutralize an opponent who's serving and volleying, make him hit the first volley from below the white band. When I return serve I watch to see if the opponent contacts the ball below the white band, and if so I move in closer, knowing I'll probably have a chance for a setup or an offensive shot. If I hit a high shot to an opponent who's at the net I have to be ready to react quickly, because he has the potential to hit an offensive shot.

7. ADVANCED D-N-O

Playing the Net

Most club players don't really understand why they should come to the net. They'll say to me, "I really don't know why I bother to go to the net. I hate it up there!" Because a player doesn't understand *why* he comes to the net, he has a fear of it and hence a lack of confidence.

The reason you come to the net to volley is to win the point. It may take a few volleys, but that's your goal up there, not to outsteady your opponent. You are on the offensive. The player who gets to the net first usually will win just because the pressure is on his opponent. The only exception is if your opponent has great passing shots, and even then, if you're serving and volleying well, the opponent won't get a decent opportunity to try a passing shot.

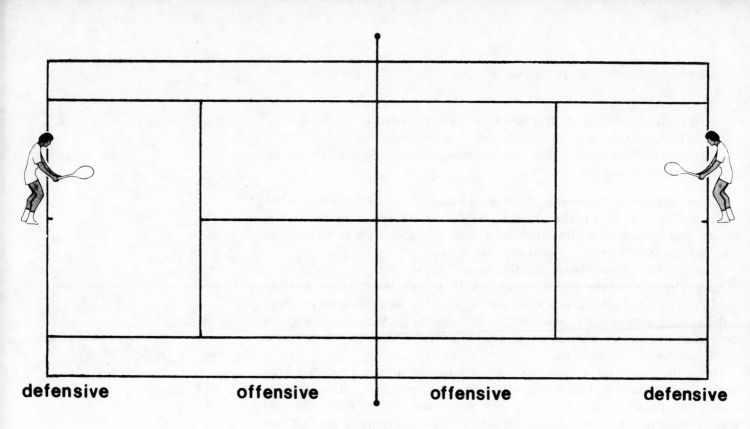

defensive　　　　**offensive**　　　　**offensive**　　　　**defensive**

NEUTRAL

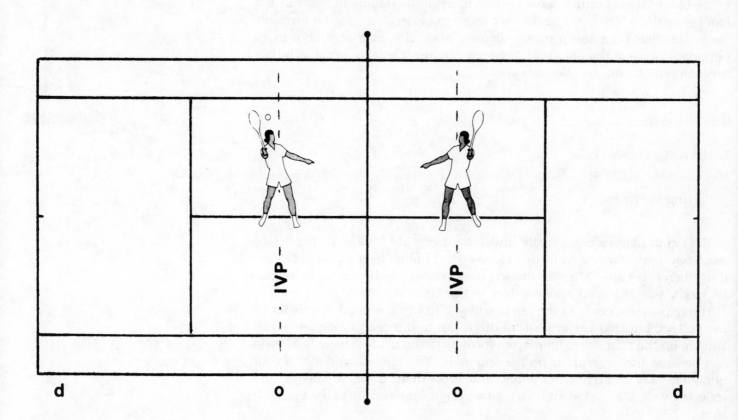

d　　　　　**o**　　　　　**o**　　　　　**d**

Diagrams 6a-b. If both players are at the baseline or both players at the net, then you have a neutral situation.

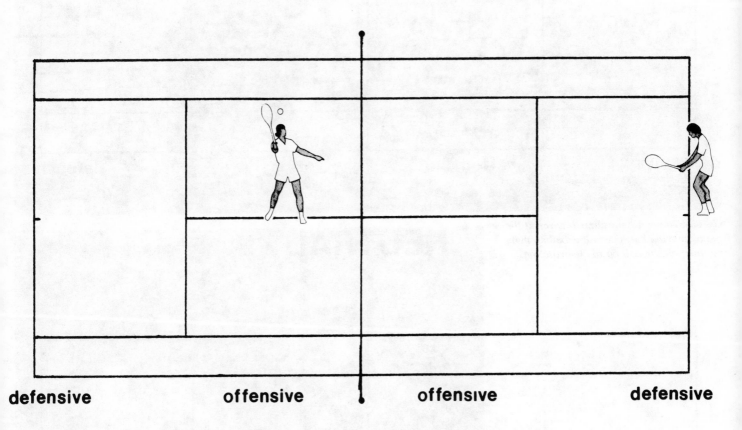

defensive   **offensive**   **offensive**   **defensive**

Diagram 6c. But, if one player is at the net and one is at the baseline, there's an offensive-defensive situation.

Fig. 63a. You can neutralize a player at the net by making him play a low ball so that he must hit the ball up to clear the net.

Fig. 63b. Contacting the ball above the white band gives a player the opportunity to hit an offensive volley.

Passing Shots

You can't hit good passing shots just by knowing how to hit a good shot. Passing shots include spin, direction, angles, and disguise. So, even players who have good groundstrokes can be pressured into frequent errors because of all the variables involved. In the first place, I'm not teaching self-coaching so you can learn to hit "winners." Most of the time a winner occurs without your really knowing it's going to occur. I never say to myself when I set up to hit a passing shot, "I'm going to hit a winner!" I have only the *potential* to hit a winner, because my opponent may simply outguess me. I may hit it perfectly down the line, but if he's standing there waiting, I've had it.

Many times a player will hit the passing shot and watch it, like Reggie Jackson watching a homer go out of the park. And then his opponent reaches out and just taps it back over, and the player is still watching his "great" passing shot that wasn't a passing shot at all. He should have moved back into position and knocked off the next one. Don't assume the point has ended when you hit a passing shot. If you hit it by him, great. If not, you've got to be prepared.

The most important thing to understand when hitting a passing shot is that you should not be trying to hit the ball deep. As long as it gets past your opponent you've hit a passing shot. Topspin is valuable then because even if the ball doesn't get past the opponent it will probably put pressure on him. If your opponent does get to it, he'll still have to make a great volley, because the ball has probably dipped at his feet.

The most common mistake a player makes when he gets a ball low at the net is trying to hit an outright winner. He thinks that because he's at the net he's in an offensive position, but a ball taken below the white band (D) at the net (O) is a neutral position (N), and that calls for a setup shot, not an outright winner.

Chip Shots

A chip shot is a backspin shot with very little pace, one that just clears the net. A chip shot is hit exactly like a backspin drive except the racquet comes through slower and the follow-through is often shortened. One of the advantages of using backspin when the opponent is at the net is that backspin creates a slower ball. If you can make your opponent play a slower ball below the white band, he'll have trouble doing anything with it.

A chip shot is useful because you can increase your variety and control with it. You can bust up someone's rhythm and you can hit very acute angles, because the ball travels much more slowly and you can more or less ease it into the short corners of the court. Backspin is your control spin, and therefore you can do more with it in terms of control than you can with topspin. Use chip shots against players who need pace to volley well or against a player who changes grips at the net. The low chip is also effective against tall players, because they often have trouble bending for low balls.

Remember, two things occur when you come to the net: (1) your opponent's errors automatically increase, and (2) he'll tend to hit the ball harder, which means his accuracy goes down. And accuracy is everything on passing shots. Until a player learns that he doesn't have to hit hard to hit a successful passing shot (he can chip or use topspin to drop the ball at the opponent's feet), the volleyer has a distinct advantage.

8. CONTACTING GROUND STROKES ABOVE THE WHITE BAND

If you contact a ball above the white band when you're at the net, your target should be one of the side T's so you can put the shot away. But if you're at the baseline, your goal is to put pressure on your opponent by putting pace on the ball. If you get a high bouncer near the baseline, do something with it, don't just get it back. You have a potential offensive shot, because you don't need much of an arc to get it over the net. So you can hit it flatter and harder and keep it in. Also, the ball will be in the air less time, which means your opponent has less time to get to the ball.

One of the easiest and yet one of the most frequently missed shots is the slow, short, high-bouncing setup somewhere inside the service line. It has "putaway" stamped all over it, and yet a player will frequently hit this shot long. That's very damaging to a player's confidence, because he has worked like crazy to force a weak shot and then he blows the putaway.

The reason this "lolly" is one of the most frequently missed shots is that it's the least practiced. It's very hard to practice properly but can be done effectively with three or four players and a ball machine (or feeder). Such a drill keeps everybody moving and creates a practical situation of approaching the net. Mechanically, it's a very simple shot, if it's practiced. Simply close the racquet face and hit behind and on *top* of the ball. If you try an excess of topspin it will involve a rotation of the wrist, which means complications and errors. So the best technique is to keep the wrist locked throughout the shot and come over the top of the ball. This causes the ball to topspin naturally.

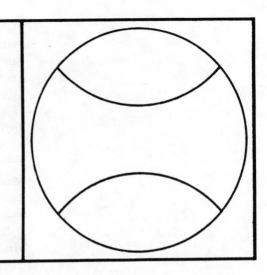

Chapter Sixteen
Match Strategy, Part III: The Wind, the Sun, and Other Problems

1. THE MOST-FEARED OPPONENTS—WIND AND SUN

Most tennis players put a high sun and gusty wind in the same category as pestilence and famine. If it's windy on the day of a match, mysterious injuries are claimed that suddenly vanish the next day. In Hawaii, where the sun is very bright and hot, there are many players who can't play between eleven and one because the sun destroys their "perfect toss." There are thousands of available excuses to latch onto in tennis: blisters, marital problems, bad-fitting shoes, too much to eat, too little to eat—the list is endless.

When I played the South African Sugar Circuit, one of the stops was Port Elizabeth, and the wind was so strong there that I once tossed the ball too high and the wind threw it back over the fence into a garage behind the court. In Beersheba, Israel, there were hundreds of kids outside the stadium and their favorite game was to loft stones inside and see if they could hit one of the players. There was always heavy wagering among these delinquents. In the South Pacific, we played on courts composed of coral, and if you fell, tournament personnel had to take a wire brush and scrape the wound clean to prevent infection. (The coral would actually grow in the wound if you left it.) This preyed heavily on my mind, particularly since the footing on coral is not the best.

So there are always plenty of problems on the court, but the worst problem you can encounter in tennis is a bad attitude. Imagine the advantage a player automatically gains if he loves playing in the wind and his opponent hates it. The match is just about over. That one mental difference will overcome nearly anything. The wind is your ally. Period. If you never say "I hate playing in the wind" again you will win 75 percent of your matches on a windy day without hitting the ball over the net, because your opponent will be concentrating so hard on his fear and loathing he will forget to hit the ball.

The wind, the sun, and the courts are your allies. When the wind is at your back you don't have to hit the ball so hard. When you're hitting against the wind you can often hit the heck out of the ball and it won't go out. A side wind will allow you to hit the ball into or away from your opponent. You can play like a king in the wind!

Always check the wind. Feel it on the back of your hands, your legs, and your face. When you play into the wind it's best to hit topspin, and when you have the wind at your back, backspin is most effective. Seldom use topspin with the wind at your back, because a topspin shot should clear the net by several feet. Since wind velocity usually increases with height, a high shot can get caught up in the wind and easily carry beyond the baseline. Backspin, though it won't dip down as quickly, can be hit lower.

A player who learns to play with natural movement instead of structured form will be able to adjust better under unusual conditions. For example, a server with a very structured toss will have trouble in the wind, but a player who learns to serve emphasizing the wrist will be able to adjust. In other words, a player who learns "contact area" and "emergencies" will be able to handle crosswinds, bad bounces, and any other problems that occur in a match.

The major problems presented by a bright, high sun are seeing the ball on the serve and overheads, and heat exhaustion. Those pros who insist that a perfect toss is mandatory for a good serve have been out in the sun too long. Or not long enough. They'll draw a circle at your feet and tell you to make the ball land in that circle. But what if the sun is at the exact spot where the toss must go to land in the circle? You may have the perfect toss, but it'll only be effective on perfect days—which means you'll only be able to hit a serve about ten days out of every year unless you play indoors or at night. You've got to learn to alter your toss on your serve, and that's largely a mental thing. Sure, a consistent toss is an asset, but as I've said before, the key to the serve is the wrist. As far as the overhead is concerned, the best thing to do if you're blinded by the sun while hitting an overhead is to let it bounce. Shielding the eyes with the left hand also helps—or wear a sun visor.

Heat exhaustion is a real peril, and the best remedy is preparation. Be sure to bring a hat, a change of shirt, lots of sweat bands, towels, and water. Also, be aware of your opponent. How is he holding up? There is a phenomenon known as "early match dizziness"—the shakes—and you can beat a far superior player if you jump on him early while he's trying to adjust to a very hot day.

Also, beware on a cold day. On a hot day you can warm up and take a break before your match, but on a cold day your practice and the match should, ideally, be back to back. Taking a break on a cold day is an easy way to court injuries and chills. Also, don't play the first couple of games in your warm-ups before you take them off. As you shed clothes for greater mobility, your sweat and the sudden cold will chill your body—a great method for getting pneumonia.

In the rarefied air at high altitudes, the ball takes off. A player who goes from the mountains to sea level to play will have less trouble keeping the ball in than usual, as long as he gets the ball over the net. But if you go from sea level to the mountains (to any altitude over 3,000 feet), which is more common, since most of us live near sea level, then you'll have trouble, especially for the first hour. The best way to adjust quickly is to aim all your shots at the service line—they'll land around the baseline. In fact, there are a few circuit players who sometimes go to train at high altitude because it builds the lung capacity and forces them to gain better control over the ball.

2. PLAYING ON DIFFERENT COURT SURFACES

Clay

The important thing on clay is to establish the frame of mind that when you walk out on the court you're going to be there for a while. There's a joke in Europe, where they play mostly on slow red clay—you take your lunch to the court. Or your dinner. Or your lunch and dinner. And it's hard for a fast-living American who's used to getting the whole match over in an hour to accept the fact that the first set may take an hour.

The mental attitude for each point is similar. You figure, "I'm going to serve and stay right here and hit balls back. And I'm not going to make any mistakes." You immediately establish the attitude that you will eliminate all mistakes. You'll do *anything* to get the ball back over the net.

I saw a match between Bill Alvarez and Eduardo Zuleta the first year I played in Europe and one point lasted twenty-seven minutes! Figuring one shot for every three seconds on clay, that point consisted of about 540 shots. You seldom hit that many shots in a whole match on concrete.

The next stage in learning to play clay-court tennis is to do something with the ball, which means using the seven target zones. The side T's are used (on clay and hard courts) for putaway volleys and as setup areas on ground strokes to maneuver the opponent outside the doubles alley. A side-T shot leaves the court wide open, and though you may not be able to hit a winner, your opponent will probably have to run a long way to get to the next shot. If your opponent counters your shots with his own placements, then it becomes like a boxing match with both players counterpunching. That's when clay-court tennis becomes very exciting.

Roy Emerson, a great clay-court player, was perhaps the fittest tennis player I've ever known. I watched him run ten miles one day—five miles forward and five backward! Running became a major part of his game. He was one of the few Australians who could win on any surface. He didn't have classic strokes, but he was fit and had great court awareness.

The thing that made Emerson really great was that he was one of the few who could serve-and-volley on clay. There's a special technique to the serve-and-volley on clay. First of all, don't serve hard. The trick is to time the speed of your serve according to your foot speed—to the speed with which you can get inside the service line and get set. (On the other hand, you can't serve too softly, either, or the opponent will pass you on the return.) If you're super-fit you can get a step or two inside the service line, which is what you have to do to serve-and-volley successfully on clay. And you must get balanced. You can't rush the net and try to stop abruptly or you'll end up on your face, because the footing is so uncertain on clay.

Hard Courts

The basic strategy on a hard court is related to the speed of the surface. And on a hard court the speed runs the gamut from as fast as ice to as slow as clay; the slower the hard court is, the more you follow clay-court strategy. If the court is very fast there are few tactics or strategies involved. So there's not much real stroke production—much of play is simply blocking the ball back. There's no such thing as finessing a guy on a very fast hard court. You seldom dropshot, and patience is not as important, because a point lasts only three or four shots. The chances of exploiting an opponent's weakness, therefore, are less on a hard court. It's also a lot more difficult to hit passing shots because the ball gets to you so much faster.

Grass Courts

Grass is an unpredictable surface, so your emphasis is on getting to the net, on volleying, on taking the ball in the air, on not letting the ball bounce. That's why the Aussies, many of whom were brought up on grass, are geared to capturing the net. On grass, simply accept the fact that you're going to get a lot of bad bounces and you'll love it.

Sadly, grass courts and grass-court tournaments are a dying phenomenon. If you ever get a chance to play on a grass court, jump at it.

Playing Indoors

Playing indoors eliminates what most players consider their two main enemies—wind and sun—and it's often easier to see the ball with the consistent indoor backgrounds. The conditions on a good indoor court can be ideal, and ideal conditions enhance concentration.

There are some problems in paradise, however. The low ceiling sometimes causes problems with the lob. Since most indoor courts are built with the top of the V-roof over the net, you must learn to lob by having the path of the racquet follow the roof line, with the apex of the arc of the ball approximately above your opponent's head. It sounds difficult but it isn't. Practice it a few times and the low ceiling won't be a problem.

Another problem with indoor play is the injuries incurred by improper warm-up. Indoor court time is expensive, so everyone wants to get right to it. That extra five minutes of play isn't worth the money you end up paying to the doctor. Be sure to warm up properly.

Perhaps the biggest drawback to playing under ideal conditions indoors, however, is the shock to your game when you play outdoors and have to face the elements again.

3. ODDBALLS AND ODDBALLERS

Lefties

How many times have you heard a player say, "I was into the second set before I realized I was playing a left-hander." The first step in handling a left-hander is to know you're playing one. The second step is getting used to him. Rod Laver lost to a number of lefties he faced in the late 60's because prior to that time he had played approximately five years in a closed pro circuit in which there were no other left-handers.

Watch next time you see a guy play a lefty and notice how often he'll serve and volley to the left-hander's forehand. It's programmed. You must almost retrain yourself to play a lefty. That's why it's good to practice with a left-hander whenever possible.

There are two main problems when playing a left-hander. First of all, the ball is spinning oddly when it comes toward you because a lefty puts spin on the ball from a different side. A lefty's topspin forehand will tend to curve into a right-hander's forehand, and his slice backhand will spin away from the righty's backhand. The only strategy to counter a lefty's spin is to be prepared.

The second main problem when playing a lefty is where you hit the ball—in particular, trying to hit to his backhand side. Your normal approach to a right-hander's vulnerable backhand plays right into a lefty's booming forehand. Another difficult adjustment is hitting backhand volleys down the line, which is not an easy shot. It's a shot you hit against a right-hander only about 10 percent of the time (because you're hitting to his forehand), but suddenly against a lefty you must hit your backhand there about 90 percent of the time. Even if you miss that shot only two or three times in a match that might be enough to lose to a player you should beat.

Unless you can hit a good slice serve, serving to a lefty's backhand can be difficult. If you're having problems, try standing two or three feet from the center stripe when serving to the deuce court. In the ad court get as close to the center stripe as possible.

Another significant area of weakness for lefties is the low forehand volley. In New Zealand one time, Tony Roche (himself a lefty) told me that lefties have trouble with that shot because a lefty's slice serve to the ad court forces a right hander to hit most of his returns down the line to a lefty's backhand volley. Therefore, lefties see very few forehand volleys and it naturally becomes a weakness. After many matches against lefties I have found this to be one of the most useful pieces of advice I ever received.

Two-handers

There is a dangerous species roaming the courts in greater numbers these days—the two-hander. There have always been two-handed players in tennis (Pancho Segura, remember, had a two-handed forehand). But since Connors' and Evert's great success with the two-handed backhand this shot is seeing its greatest popularity.

The two-hander is a young person's shot. It provides extra strength to weak wrists and arms, but it also requires greater physical exertion. Because of the limitations of reach, a two-handed player must take an extra step or two to hit the ball well. With a one-handed shot, if you're stretched out, you can still get off a decent shot even though your arm is fully extended. But to supply any force at all, a two-handed shot must be hit with the arms bent. All those extra steps add up to 30 to 40 percent more running. So, to hit a two-handed shot effectively you'd better be in top physical shape—which usually means youth.

To beat a two-hander, then, make him stretch for shots. Use the side T's to run him wide, and unless he's very quick and extremely fit, he'll be an old man by the second set. Also, an effective strategy is to hit the ball high and directly at the two-hander, because the left hand on the racquet inhibits the movement of both his arms toward the right side of his body. This shot is especially effective when the two-hander is in an emergency situation and has no time to move and take the ball on his forehand.

Perhaps a two-hander's greatest weakness, however, is a low volley. A two-hander usually holds the racquet with two Eastern or Semi-Western

Forehands, and therefore to get the racquet into the open position to volley a low ball upward, the wrists must turn into an awkward position. The first thing I do when I get a two-hander as a student is to teach him how to volley with a Continental grip, because to volley with a Western or Eastern Forehand, even with the support of two hands, is a very difficult task. Most two-handers are poor volleyers. Bjorn Borg, the best player in the world, is a weak volleyer relative to most pros, and so are Harold Solomon and Eddie Dibbs. The exception to the rule is Frew McMillan, who uses two hands on *both* sides and is a *great* volleyer.

Spin Artists

When a ball is spinning it will alter its normal course when it lands—either bounce higher or lower, or left or right. When the ball has the potential to alter course it means you won't be able to predict many times what it will do. That's an emergency, so against a spin artist, shorten your backswing. Don't try to overpower a spin artist—try to outmaneuver him.

Try to bring a spin artist to the net, because he usually *hates* the net. A spin artist usually doesn't have great volleys or overheads—he just tries to get the ball back in. In fact, he seldom has power in *any* stroke and so he has developed his spin game to compensate for his lack of strength. Of course, there are players who can hit soft and hard—blast it or finesse it. If you meet a player like that—I offer my sympathies.

The Blaster

The opposite of the spin artist is the blaster—the guy who has to hit every ball as hard as he can. A good player does not hit every ball as hard as he can, so this is usually an intermediate or beginning player. A big ego and total lack of understanding of the game are his chief trademarks.

A blaster usually wins because he bores you to death. You may or may not hit a ball all day. To beat him, hang tight. That is, squeeze tight on the racquet with the bottom three fingers so the racquet doesn't fly out of your hand, and utilize minimum potential. Just block everything back. Don't try to hit harder than he does even if he calls you a sissy because you won't "hit like a man." Just play your game, Mary.

After you beat him several times, he'll take up karate again.

Chapter Seventeen
Post-game Strategy

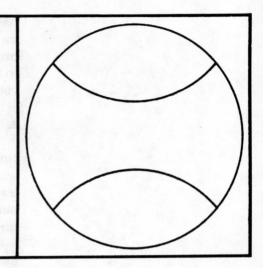

1. LEARNING FROM A LOSS

Go to any tournament and ask a player who just won what he learned from the match and he'll give you about a thirty-second answer. Then ask the player who just lost and you'll get tennis' version of the filibuster. We human beings, regrettably, seem to learn only from our losses. Winning is such a big deal in our lives that we forget *how* we won. One of the most difficult things in life is to be riding the crest of an ego wave and still maintain perspective. When you lose a match you were challenged. You were called upon to do things you couldn't do. So you find out what's wrong with your game when you lose.

To play on the higher levels of tennis or to continue to improve you must have a purpose and a goal every time you step out on the court. You must challenge yourself even when you're playing your little sister or hitting against the backboard. Because just as a stroke needs drilling and practice, your concentration on the goals of tennis must be honed.

I don't mean go out there and crush your ten-year-old daughter. I mean concentrate on perfecting a certain point of your game—play only her strength and your weakness, even if you lose. Think at all times. Challenge yourself at all times. Enjoy the game at all times. If you're bored with a match it's your own fault, because there's always something you can do to challenge yourself on the court. You should play every point of your tennis life with some purpose, and when the big points come you'll be ready for the challenge.

Often the most valuable experience in a loss is finding out there's someone better than you. So, often I'll see players who have enormous egos about their games—for no logical reason. They're number one at the Yazoo Playground and they think Connors is in trouble. Or how about the top guy at the club who's never entered a tournament outside the club (because he knows he'd get annihilated) but the size of his ego would rival the Goodyear blimp. These players find the level they can dominate and never venture out of it, because they don't want to go through the ego problem of a loss. They never challenge themselves.

When you're behind in a match, you have to examine your game. If you're being blown away mercilessly by a classy player, you usually find out you've got a lot to learn. But if you're in the trenches with some guy and every point has been a battle, but your strokes seem to falter when the pressure gets too much, then you must adjust, you must change your game. And you have to understand the game before you can change your game, before you can get to the next level. The more advanced you are mentally, the more possibilities you have to change a losing game.

2. LEARNING TO WIN

Once they get ahead, most players, instead of thinking "How am I going to win?" start wondering "How am I going to avoid losing?" So few players ever learn how to win. Winning is being able to take a 6-4, 5-4 match and close it out. Many players at that point think, "I've got a chance to win. All I've got to do is get four points."

I once saw Rod Laver play a match at Forest Hills and when he got ahead 6-4, 5-4 all the Aussies got up and started to leave. And there was this great match going on. So I looked over at Newcombe and said, "Where are you guys going?" And John answered, "Laver never blows a match at 6-4, 5-4 when he's serving." And bang, four straight points and Laver shook hands.

I watched Laver for years on the circuit. He knew how to close out a match better than anyone in the world, and all the other players realized it. It became critical to hold serve at 4-all against Laver. Against other players you had a chance to break back and even things, but against Laver it was almost always over. When you've got that feeling about an opponent it puts a lot of pressure on you. Laver would win matches just because the opponent tried so hard to hold serve at 4-all that he crumbled.

In order to make a breakthrough you must deal with a lot of intangibles. For a beginner, for example, there are no techniques for closing out a match. It has to be intangibles—determination, drive, motivation, or just running harder. And the biggest breakthrough is confidence. Confidence can come from within, but most often it comes from without, from positive reinforcements—having a good coach, a good friend, or a good experience, like winning.

If you're on a losing streak it's often a good idea to play in lesser tournaments or against lesser opponents and learn how to win again—build up confidence and the winning attitude. On the circuit I often played local weekend city tournaments (I was usually out of the pro tournament by then) where I knew I could get to the semis or the finals and probably win. Then I'd go back to the circuit and I'd be much sharper because I'd developed a winning attitude. Losing is so often just a frame of mind. You've got to break that frame of mind and learn the trick of winning.

3. SET REALISTIC GOALS

The first critical step to improving is to set a realistic goal. Often players will watch the pros on TV and they figure, "I'll do it that way." But you can't really copy the pros. You can't make those running backhand passing shots, drop volleys, or heavy topspin lobs unless you've totally committed yourself to playing tennis as they have. Totally committed! That means give up your job and play tennis eight hours a day, run, eat right, get your brains beat out, and, for most of us, turn back the clock ten, twenty, thirty, or forty years.

Most people are not going to play professional tennis. You've got to understand who you are and where you are—not just where you are in life but where you are in the match and on the court. Your goal must be realistic or you're headed for a lot of frustration. If you want to be on the circuit in two years and you just started the game last week at thirty-five, that's not being realistic. The greatest stumbling block to improvement is frustration—not a lousy backhand or poor conditioning. People usually don't quit playing tennis because their backhand stinks but because they're frustrated. They've set unrealistic goals that they have no chance of reaching.

You may have the idea that if you tell everybody in town you're going to be on the pro circuit in three years it will push you on to greater heights. But all you're really doing is setting up a situation in which you'll look bad. On the other hand, don't put yourself down. Climbing a 10,000-foot mountain is a great accomplishment, but if you compare it to Sir Edmund Hillary's feat it'll seem like a stroll around Piccadilly. Hillary had a retinue and money and supplies and years of training, which is exactly what Connors had on his climb to the top.

Frustration does not come from setting up a goal and striving for it. Frustration comes from always setting up goals that you have no chance of attaining—in other words, constantly creating no-win situations in which you will always be frustrated. People who set impossible goals are the people who eventually give up tennis.

Remember, you're like 99 percent of all humans—it'll take you a little while to make corrections. It'll take some time.

4. PLAYING HAPPY

Have you ever watched a great tennis match and then been charged up to go out and play? Your first five or six games are often unbelievable because you're on a high—you're inspired. Can you imagine how you'd play if you could maintain that level of excitement for tennis at all times?

I've always admired Jimmy Connors' enthusiasm. He's just bubbling with enthusiasm for the game of tennis. He had that same excitement for the game when he was a kid playing on the back courts. He just bounces, and he carries it on to center court. He is one of the few players in the modern era who truly loves playing tennis and competing.

If players could maintain enthusiasm they could improve. Often the guy who plays twice a week can improve faster than the guy who plays five times a week because he's more eager. You can improve faster playing hard for one hour a day than going through the motions for six hours. Connors is one of the hardest practicers on the circuit, and yet often he'll only practice for forty-five minutes or so. But when he comes off the court he's dripping from head to toe with sweat and his practice partner is exhausted. As soon as you lose your enthusiasm during a practice it's better to just stop.

Many players today have lost the attitude that tennis is fun to play. Play happy. Have a good attitude. When you're out there grumbling next time, snap yourself out of it. Play happy and you'll love the game, you'll love your enthusiasm, and you'll improve because of it. Just your own sheer enjoyment of the game can catapult you over the man who fights himself on every point.

5. COMMITMENT

To improve you must have a commitment—a commitment to practice, to understand the game, and to change your game if necessary. Many times a player is looking for a quick cure when he comes to a pro, and instead he gets a quick shuffle. Often he's getting what he deserves. It takes a firm commitment to improve—not just a once-a-week lesson and lots of complaining in between. Often a student will come to me for a lesson, then return seven days later and be frustrated in his next lesson. So I'll ask, "How much did you practice?" and he'll reply, "Well, I haven't had a chance."

Commitment can enable you to defeat the limitations of your body, to go beyond what is considered your potential. Most players have the illusion, however, that if you simply practice long enough you will reach that potential. But practice can actually make your game *decline*. There are only two things you can practice—bad habits and good habits. Many people regress in life because they practice bad habits, and that pattern is transferred to the tennis court.

It's the quality of your practice and the quality of your understanding that determine if you will improve. And maintaining a high quality for a sustained period of time is most important. One day of practice every other month will not help, because, among other things, what you practice today often won't show in your game for several months. So you've got to keep at it.

The typical club player won't practice if the day isn't perfect. If it's too windy or too hot or he doesn't feel that good he doesn't even consider practicing. You'll often hear him say, "My game gets worse when I practice in the wind," which means when the day isn't just perfect he can't play a match because he's never practiced in those conditions.

Another bad idea most players harbor is that they have to find someone better than they are to practice with or the practice is useless. But actually, in many cases, you should sometimes practice with weaker players, especially if you want to work on something, because a strong player usually won't give you that chance—unless you want to work on chasing balls. You may be more enthusiastic when you play a better player and your game will pick up accordingly. But if you're not enthusiastic—unless you play someone who can tromp on you—then it's not your game that needs work, it's your attitude. If I'm working on my game I always like to practice with a woman. In fact, on the circuit I often preferred practicing with women because the men often hit ridiculously hard. The slightly slower but steadier strokes of a woman player enabled me to perfect my timing. The first time I practiced with Chris Evert, for example, after twelve minutes I still had two brand-new balls in my pocket. If she is a consistent hitter there is no better way to perfect your strokes than practicing with a woman.

Practice with the same intensity that you play with, because the way you practice is inevitably the way you will play. The quality of your preparation for match play is based on what and how you practice. That's why you never see a player just play matches and do well—no one can. There's a mental preparation also that has to go into a good practice. If you stay out late and struggle through practice you're not committed.

Most players' practice is a waste of time because they practice without a purpose. Without a sense of purpose there is no meaning to your practice. In other words, when you step out on the court for a big match or for just another practice, you must have a plan. A plan, a sense of purpose, heightens your awareness of what you can or cannot do—if you can't do it in practice, there's no hope of doing it in a match. So, when setting up drills for practice, simulate what might happen in a game. Go for the target zones, never let a ball bounce twice, run your partner around, and chase down everything he hits.

6. THE FINAL STRATEGY IS GUTS

When your strokes have fallen apart and your body is cramped or starting to cramp and your main desire is just to lie down or get a drink of water, you've got to rely on guts. Most players don't know how to transcend the physical and mental problems that bombard them. What distinguishes all great athletes is that they can draw upon a reserve. In the last few games of a five-set match there isn't a lot of classic form or strategy—it's mostly guts and desire.

First, you must realize that if you're tired your opponent is probably tired. Even if he's doing a good job of hiding his fatigue, no human being can stay out on a court for three hours under punishing conditions and not feel exhaustion setting in. When fatigue sets in, a player cramps, not only physically, but mentally. His entire mental focus is on the physical, so his concentration wanders from the court. *Never let your opponent know you're tired.* Don't let your head droop; don't lean on your racquet. Make a point of being first off the chair, and walk faster than normal. Once he thinks you're tired, what does he have to fear?

Having guts is experience—you can *develop* a gutsy attitude. Those who go the distance learn to deal with the different stresses involved with fatigue. I learned, for example, a breathing technique to use after a long grueling point. Instead of the normal reaction of taking huge gulping breaths of air (which causes hyperventilation), I would exhale several quick short breaths without inhaling any air. This reduces the level of carbon dioxide in your system (which causes shortness of breath), and you're then able to recover from oxygen deprivation four or five times more quickly.

If you never push yourself, if you refuse to do anything that doesn't feel comfortable, how will you ever know your limits? Remember, you should always have a game strategy and a backup strategy, but when those both fail, the final strategy is guts.

7. THERE ARE NO MENTAL LIMITATIONS

A great mistake club players make is trying to attain the physical level of the great players they watch on TV. Instead they should try to attain the pros' *mental* level. Physically, few can match a Borg or a Connors, because they have dedicated their lives to their physical perfection. But most players have the potential to realize their superior mental level.

My supposition is that every player in the world can be a great player mentally. Teaching pros often say that concepts such as anticipation and disguise are too advanced for the club player to learn. That's nonsense—the mind is ready. It just might take a while to sink in.

That's why a player at thirty-five can continue to improve even though his physical peak has come and gone. He can outthink other players. Also, he has come to understand what he can actually do physically on the court. He has fewer illusions. He may not be as fast as he was at twenty-five, but he can hit the ball better because he understands more about himself and the game.

If you're on the same level as your opponent, the reason for winning is intangible—glory, satisfaction, excitement over winning. My greatest accomplishments on the court came not on days when I hit every ball in the middle of the strings and blew my opponent off the court, but on the days when I had to scrape and dig for every point, when I used my entire physical and mental capabilities, when I was outplayed and still managed to win. Those are the days I still remember.

8. CONCLUSION: UNDERSTANDING *YOUR* OWN GAME

Creative players create the future of tennis. Because most tennis players were locked into conventional form they stalled their own future and the future of the game. Release yourself from the prison of form. Release yourself from the fear of not looking good. Form is fine if you understand why you hit the ball that way, but most players copy form because it looks good. They have no idea why they hit the ball the way they do. Tennis is a game invented and developed by people—there is no God-given right or wrong. There is only what works. Try whatever you want as long as you don't injure yourself or hopelessly handicap your progress. And the way to prevent that is to get a clear understanding of tennis.

To get to the next level you must understand what the next level is. You must know where you're headed or you'll never get there. That means you must have some perspective on the game in general and your own game in particular. Understanding is your road map. This is not a "how-to" book. This is a book of understanding. I purposely avoided telling you specifically how to hit the ball because there is no right way to hit the ball. Even in the sections on hitting strokes (Phases Two and Three) the emphasis is on understanding what happens to the ball when your racquet does certain things—not how to hit that stroke "correctly."

Your goal should be to gain enough understanding so that you can eventually become your own coach. If you study this book, diligently practice the drills, and constantly implement the techniques of self-coaching, you will immediately begin to improve, and in a couple months you will be off the level that you've been stuck on for years. And when your friends begin to remark about your improvement, don't tell them Burwash said to do this or that. Tell them that you finally understand what you're doing on the court. Tell them you finally understand tennis.

Phase Five
A Guide for the Health-conscious Tennis Player

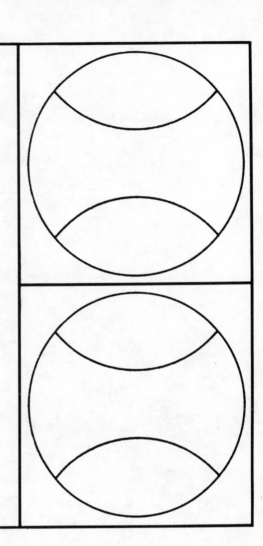

Chapter Eighteen
Shaping Up

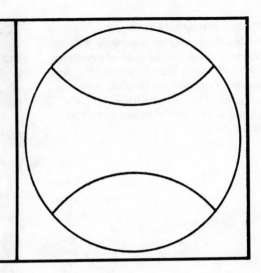

You sometimes hear a player say, "I was in the zone today. I could do no wrong, I really felt great." We've all had these days. The problem is—not often enough. Well, whether you've realized it or not, those are often the days when you're feeling extra-healthy. If you want to make a breakthrough in your tennis game, make a breakthrough in your health. If you're carrying thirty or forty extra pounds, or if your muscles are in poor condition from lack of exercise, you'll probably never be a good tennis player.

Many players need basic lessons in health more than they need tennis lessons. The simple fact is that if your body is not in tune, it's hard to tune up your game. You've got to eat and sleep right and exercise your entire body regularly.

1. INJURY PREVENTION

Most injuries in tennis can be related to improper warm-up or conditioning. Ankle sprains and knee injuries occur with the greatest frequency to players who haven't participated in any exercise in months and then jump right out on the court and try to go full blast. And a major cause of sore arms is the FBI. You know—"first ball in." A player won't take any warm-up serves, then he tries to blast the first few serves 100 mph and he wonders why his arm just fell off. Most injuries are caused by foolishness, not weakness. The majority of injuries can be avoided by proper conditioning and flexibility.

2. FIVE WAYS TO GET TENNIS ELBOW

There are five basic ways of getting tennis elbow:

1. Placing the Thumb Behind the Grip for More Support on Backhands

When you place your thumb behind the racquet handle on backhands, the tendency is to point the elbow out toward the ball and "push" at the ball from the elbow (see Figs. 64a-b). This makes the elbow the *center of rotation*. But properly, the swing should start at the shoulder, not the elbow, because the shoulder is a rollable ("ball and socket") joint capable of the rotation necessary to swing the arm. The elbow, however, is a bendable joint, and the

Fig. 64a. Hitting backhands with the thumb behind the handle or "thumb up the back" is one of the principal ways of developing tennis elbow, as the elbow becomes the center of rotation for the shot. Anatomically, the elbow is a bendable joint and should not be forced to become a rotational joint.

Fig. 64b. A player who leads with his elbow usually has an incorrect grip (either a forehand grip or his thumb behind the handle). This puts strain on the elbow joint and is an excellent way to develop tennis elbow.

strain caused when a player swings from the elbow is one of the chief causes of tennis elbow. In order to prevent undue strain on the arm, which may lead to injury, the thumb should be a nonfunctional digit on the backhand.

2. Straightening the Arm on a Forehand

I'm amazed that even today so many players are still hitting their forehands with a straight arm. Because of a lack of understanding of anatomy, they're setting themselves up for a likely arm injury. On contacting the ball, force is transferred from the wrist to the elbow. If the arm is bent, the biceps, the main stabilizing muscles of the arm, are working, and the force is transferred along the biceps to the shoulder joint, which is capable of absorbing this shock. When the arm is straight, however, the biceps are relaxed (the triceps have taken over) and the force stops in the elbow region. This continual shock to the elbow joint will usually result in injury (see Figs. 65a-b).

3. Serving with a Straight Arm and a Firm Wrist

Once again, if the arm is straight the biceps have extended fully and all the shock transfers from the wrist to the elbow.

If you're having trouble snapping your wrist, release the last three fingers of the racquet completely and grip the racquet with only the thumb and forefinger (see Fig. 66). Since the last three fingers control the tendons, which tighten the wrist, this will ensure a loose wrist.

4. Whipping Topspin

One of the most common causes of tennis elbow is trying to put excessive topspin on the ball when hitting ground strokes by rolling over the top of the ball with the wrist and elbow. Again, this is asking the elbow to act as a rollable joint, which it cannot do without risk of injury (see Fig. 67).

5. Bad Timing

The final basic way of getting tennis elbow is plain old bad timing. Mishitting the ball because of bad timing strains the muscles and joints the same way unexpectedly missing a stairstep can wrench you. The ball comes through faster or slower than you thought and the resulting mishit causes a tearing of muscle tissue.

This problem is much more prevalent among men than women. Men usually try to pound the ball long before they have the timing perfected. The best remedy is to simply stop swinging so hard. Slow down. Pretend your arm is in a slow-motion movie.

3. CONDITIONING EXERCISES

One of the nice advantages of tennis is that it's a great overall fitness sport. Playing a lot of tennis can eliminate the necessity for lots of detailed exercises. There are, however, certain areas of the body that need special attention for you to play better tennis.

Fig. 65a. Hitting with a straight arm on the forehand is also a good way to develop tennis elbow.

Fig. 65b. To help prevent tennis elbow, forehands should be hit with a bent arm. This not only helps relieve pressure on the elbow, but allows for greater flexibility when playing in the wind or with balls that take a funny hop or are hit into you.

Fig. 66. Even when the hand touches the racquet, the grip should be loose while serving. Some top players keep their last three fingers completely off the racquet during the serve. This helps you keep a loose flexible wrist.

Fig. 67. Rolling the racquet over the ball to create more topspin is an excellent way to develop tennis elbow. This is an unnatural motion for the arm. Topspin occurs naturally by hitting from low to high with your racquet head coming through perpendicular to the ground.

After conversations with many doctors and fitness experts and years of personal experience with pros and students I found there are three parts of the body that particularly need strengthening for tennis—the wrists, the ankles, and the stomach muscles.

Strengthening the Wrists

The tendons and muscles of the wrist must be strong, because it's the wrist that connects the racquet to the rest of the body. And the wrist becomes particularly important in emergency situations and when executing many of the more advanced "touch" shots that take a firm but flexible wrist.

To strengthen the wrists, do "rope rolls." Tie one end of a rope about four feet long to the middle of a stick about eighteen inches long. Tie the other end of the rope to a one-pound weight. Then, with one hand on either end of the stick, wind the weight up from the ground to the stick by rolling the rope around the stick. Then back down again. Repeat several times.

Keeping the Ankles Strong and Flexible

The ankle is very injury-prone, because it is the joint closest to the ground and so takes the most pounding. Most ankle injuries are caused because the ankle is not strong and flexible at the same time. Usually, the tendon will snap because it has not been prestretched. So, special attention should be given to stretching the ankle (see the section below on stretching).

Strengthening the Stomach Muscles

Just about every movement in tennis, including the serve, the overhead, and the ground strokes, initiates from the stomach. Since the bellybutton is the center of gravity, strength and control of the abdomen is a key to almost every phase of the game. You'll be quicker off the mark with a smaller, tighter, more muscular stomach. The whipping motion of the arm on the serve actually starts at the stomach. And when you're in the air hitting an overhead, any power must come from the stomach.

"Cross-body" situps are the best exercise for strengthening a "jelly-belly." Lie on your back and bring your knees up until your feet are flat on the ground. Then alternately lift up and touch your right elbow to your left knee, back down, then touch the left elbow to your right knee. Start with a reasonable number of repetitions and build up from there.

4. SHAPING UP THE LEGS

To get the legs in shape for tennis, I don't recommend jogging. There's nothing wrong with jogging. It's great exercise and also helps build your wind, but it is not the best sort of running for tennis. I recommend instead "shuttle runs."

Place one racquet on the ground at the net with ten balls on the strings, and one racquet at the baseline (without the balls). Then, starting at the baseline, transfer all ten balls, one at a time, to the racquet at the baseline. This start-and-stop-and-bending motion is identical to what your legs go through in a match.

Other excellent exercises for developing stamina and strength in the legs are skipping rope and playing lots of mini-tennis.

5. STRETCHING AND FLEXIBILITY

Flexibility is the range of possible movement in a joint or series of joints (when the spinal column is involved). The need for flexibility varies with the sport. In tennis, because of the demands put on every part of the body, it is all-important. Even for the armchair athlete, flexibility is important just to walk correctly. An improper gait caused by stiffness results many times in lower-back problems—and maintaining flexibility prevents or relieves the aches and pains that grow common with age and often foreshadow arthritis.

Basically there are three reasons why we need to stretch our muscles: (1) to improve our range of motion, (2) to help relieve muscle soreness after physical overexertion, and (3) to help prevent injury (as by loosening up your ankles before a match to prevent strains).

There are two types of stretching exercises: (1) the dynamic or ballistic, in which bobbing, bouncing, and jerky movements are used, and (2) the static method, which involves holding a static position for a set period of time while locking the joints involved into a position. That places the muscles and connective tissue at their greatest possible length.

Both methods satisfactorily stretch the muscles, but there are three distinct advantages to static stretching. First, there is less danger of overstretching muscle tissue. Remember that the muscles are like rubber bands. If you continue to pull on a rubber band in quick, jerky motions, it probably will break (like tearing a muscle), but if you gradually stretch the rubber band, you will eventually feel the limit of its elasticity. In static stretching, this is where you hold the position. Second, in static stretching you use less energy because there is less motion. Third, ballistic stretching often causes muscular soreness, whereas static stretching can actually relieve it.

Pre-tennis Stretching Exercises

The following stretching exercises can be done before you play tennis, to help loosen up your muscles and avoid injury.

You can expand these exercises for a more comprehensive stretching program designed to improve your overall flexibility.

1a. Stretching the calf muscles. Stand, feet together, approximately one racquet's length away from the net post, with your hands resting on the post and your arms slightly bent (see Fig. 68a). Keeping your heels on the ground and your legs straight, lower your hips toward the post. When you feel the stretch in your calves, hold the position for thirty seconds. Relax and repeat once.

1b. Stretching the Achilles tendons. Starting from the same position with heels on the ground, bend your knees forward toward the net post (see Fig. 68b). When you feel the stretch in your Achilles tendons, hold the position for thirty seconds. Relax and repeat once.

2. Stretching the quadriceps and ankles. Place your left hand on the net post for balance and bend your right leg up behind you. With your right hand, grasp your toes and pull up until you feel the stretch (see Fig. 69). Hold the position for thirty seconds. Do the same exercise with the left leg. Repeat once for each leg.

Fig. 69. Stretching the quadriceps and
ankles.

3. Stretching the ankles. Using the net post for balance, raise your right foot off the ground slightly and slowly rotate the foot at the ankle in a circle for thirty seconds (see Figs. 70a-c). Do the same with the left foot.

4. Stretching the buttocks. Standing upright, lift the right leg, bending it at the knee. Grasp the right leg just below the knee, using both hands with fingers interlocked (see Fig. 71). Pull the leg upwards, hold for two seconds, then switch legs. Repeat for each leg five times.

5a. Stretching the hamstrings and lower back. Sit on a bench, left leg down beside you and right leg straight out on the bench in front of you. Keeping your right leg straight and your toes pointed forward, lean toward the foot with your arms extended. Touch the toe if possible, or whatever point you can reach without straining (see Fig. 72a). Eventually your head may also touch your knee. Hold the position for thirty seconds.

5b. Stretching the hamstrings, lower back, and calves. Starting from the same position on the bench, flex the foot with the toes pointing upward. Do the exercise as before (see Fig. 72b). Eventually you will be able to hold onto the foot and pull the toes toward you. Repeat both exercises 5a and 5b with the left leg.

6. Stretching the muscles on the side of the body. Stand with your feet apart, both arms above your head holding the racquet. Bend to the right until you feel the stretch along your side (see Fig. 73). Hold for five seconds and then bend to the left. Repeat three times on both sides.

7. Stretching the shoulders, upper arms, and back. Hold the racquet behind your back with both hands. Bend forward, keeping the arms and legs straight, and allow the arms to extend upward and forward (see Fig 74). Hold this position for ten seconds, relax, and repeat three times.

8. Stretching the shoulders, upper arms, and back. Holding the racquet in your right hand, allow it to hang down your back. Grasp the throat of the racquet with your left hand and pull the racquet down, pointing the right elbow to the sky (see Fig. 75). Hold this position for thirty seconds, then do the exercise with the left arm. Repeat once for both arms.

a.

b.

c.

Fig. 71. Stretching the buttocks.

Fig. 72a. Stretching the hamstrings and lower back.

Fig. 72b. Stretching the hamstrings, lower back, and calves.

Fig. 73. Stretching the muscles on the side of the body.

Fig. 74. Stretching the shoulders, upper arms, and back.

Fig. 75. Stretching the shoulders, upper arms, and back.

Chapter Nineteen
Eating Right

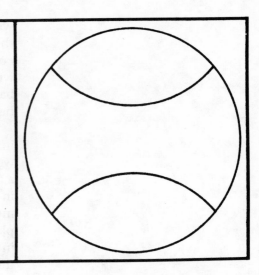

1. THE VEGETARIAN FUGITIVE

One day in 1971, when I was in between circuits, I was throwing a Frisbee around on the beach in Waikiki with a bunch of my friends and accidentally hit a guy on the head with the Frisbee. I went over to apologize and it turned out he was a doctor and was in town attending a medical symposium on diets—the essence of which was that meat was the worst thing you could put in your body. Oh, no! *Vegetarians!*

I have always tried to live by the idea that an intelligent person has an open mind and a closed-minded person learns nothing. But to tell the truth, I had a preconceived notion of a vegetarian as a kind of scrawny know-it-all. I remember thinking I wanted to get back to the Frisbee, but I felt obliged to sit there and listen to this guy because I'd bopped him on the head. So he started drawing charts in the sand and telling me that an athlete should not eat meat six months before an event. Finally, he persuaded me I should show up at the symposium. But I wasn't exactly convinced.

In the first place, vegetarianism was totally foreign to me. I was brought up a hockey player. A big, juicy, rare steak was a reward and preparation for battle all at once. I needed some moral support. So I went with seven of my friends—five guys and two girls. We showed up at the Hilton Hawaiian Village Convention Hall, where there were 300 doctors all in suits and ties. And here come eight beach bums—barefooted, wearing bathing suits, and hauling surfboards. We sat way in the back by the door with the surfboards propped up against the wall so we could get out of there fast. We'd all made a deal that as soon as it got boring we'd head back to the beach. Total estimated time was about five minutes.

Five *hours* later, after dozens of speakers and demonstrations and statistics and studies and tests, after the very last speaker, we finally left. We all went "cold turkey" off meat, and not one of us has touched a piece of meat, fish, poultry, or eggs since. That's how convinced we were.

But the real clincher came when I went to Lloyd Percival's Fitness Center in Toronto, Canada. He had a fitness program in which he tested all of the top athletes in the country. From 1967 to 1969 I was between number fifty and number sixty in the country as a meat eater. The year I stopped eating meat I really wanted to do well in the test, because by then I'd become a "vegetarian fugitive." I refused to discuss my eating habits or go out to dinner with anyone because I was embarrassed to be a vegetarian. My parents thought I'd gone off the deep end, and all the players on the circuit constantly ribbed me. I remember I was playing once and Marty Riessen, with whom I played doubles in South Africa, yelled out at me after I missed a ball, "Hey, Burwash, you'd be a lot faster if you didn't have so many carrots hanging out of your ears." And Riessen was one of the *nice* guys.

So I was very anxious to do well on that fitness test. I had to at least score in the top sixty again so I wouldn't look like a complete idiot—but the cards were stacked against me that day. The day before I had to play in the finals of a tournament in St. Petersburg, Florida. Billie Jean King and Chris Evert were in the women's finals right before me, and they had a long match. Then I got into a long match myself and missed my plane for Toronto. So I got a late plane to Cleveland and ended up sleeping on a bench at the Hopkins airport in Cleveland so I would catch the seven A.M. flight to Toronto. When I got off the plane in Toronto I went right to the Fitness Center, and I felt the way anyone would feel if they'd slept that night on a bench in an airport—totally exhausted. And the testing procedure was fourteen hours long.

About halfway through the tests this doctor burst into my room and screamed, "What have you been doing?" And I figured, "Geez, I've blown it now." But then he said, "You've improved 20 percent in this area and 50 percent in that area and 38 percent in this area." I figured here was another guy who was going to give me static about being a vegetarian, and suddenly he was giving me proof that I was right all along. After a year of being a vegetarian fugitive, those were sweet words.

I had significantly improved my score in every area tested. And the only change I'd made was in my diet. After one year as a vegetarian I had the highest fitness index of any athlete in the country, and I remained number one every year I was tested.

I wasn't training, I didn't run, I'd just been playing my regular tournament schedule, and I was traveling a lot, which is a great strain on the body. But the testing showed that I was the single most fit athlete of those being tested.

I wanted to present my own experience with a meatless diet to you so that you might give it some thought. At one time vegetarianism was totally foreign to me, and I have always been grateful to the man who introduced it to me. Vegetarianism changed my life, made me healthier, happier, and a better tennis player, with more energy and stamina and a better mental outlook. But it also gave me insights that opened up a whole new way of thinking for me and changed my life in ways I never thought it would.

I personally don't eat any meat, but if this seems extreme, then at least, for the health of your body, cut down on your intake of meat.

2. HINTS FOR A HEALTHY DIET

Eating a sensible, varied diet, be it meatless or low-meat, while avoiding "empty calories" and excessive sugar and saturated fats, should keep your body working, and playing, at its best. Here are some basic nutritional guidelines.

Eat as many fresh fruits and vegetables as possible. Avoid processed or canned foods—you never know what's in them. If you do buy food that is packaged, make sure you read the label. Check for additives like chemical coloring, flavoring and preservatives, and sugar.

Use whole-wheat flour and whole-grain breads and cereals. So-called enriched white flour has most of the food value removed and only about one-sixth replaced. Why take in empty calories—calories with no nutritional value?

Avoid added sugar. For example, refined white sugar and foods "enriched" with it act destructively on the body, leaching it of vitamins and minerals. Brown sugar is just white sugar covered with molasses. A little honey in recipes isn't bad—but, if possible, reeducate your tastes. Sugar is sugar.

Swear off junk foods and beverages. It might not be easy, but once you start reading what's actually in these "fabricated foods," it should make you more resolved.

Be sensible in your intake of saturated fats. Research shows that they contribute to high cholesterol. Saturated fats are usually of animal origin, and some examples are meat, egg yolks, butter, and cheese. This doesn't mean that your diet should be free of all cholesterol and saturated fats—only that you should keep them at a sensible level.

3. A WORD ABOUT PROTEIN

Protein is essential to the body for growth and repair. During digestion the protein is broken down into units called amino acids, of which eight are essential to good health. A "complete" protein contains all eight of these essential amino acids. Two "incomplete" proteins will complement each other, and when eaten in combination give the body a better source of protein than some complete proteins can do.

Most people seem aware of the protein in meat, eggs, and dairy products, but protein is also obtained from grains, nuts, seeds, and legumes, like beans, peas, and lentils. There is even protein in fruits and non-legume vegetables.

Some food groups which combine well to make excellent sources of protein are grains and dairy products (for example, cereal and milk); grains and legumes (for example, bread and peanut butter—peanuts are actually legumes); legumes and seeds (for example, the soy flour and sunflowers combined in granola).

4. SUGGESTED RECIPES

Meals should be as varied and creative as they are nutritious. Whether you are considering a meatless diet or just a few more meatless meals, these recipes might offer some new ideas to you. Or maybe spark your own culinary creativity.

BREAKFAST

GRANOLA

5 cups rolled oats
1 cup sunflower seeds
1 cup sliced or slivered almonds
1 cup shredded or chipped coconut
    (unsweetened)
½ cup sesame seeds (unhulled)
½ cup wheat germ
½ cup bran
½ cup soy flour
½ cup powdered milk
1 cup vegetable oil
1 cup honey
¾ cup raisins

Combine all but last 3 ingredients, and mix. Stir together the oil and honey, and add to dry ingredients. Mix well. Spread into lightly greased 9- by 13-inch pan. Bake at 350 degrees for about 45 minutes, stirring every 10 to 15 minutes. Add the raisins in the last 5 minutes.

Store in airtight container. Serve with milk. This granola is exceptionally high in protein, even before serving with milk. It contains a dairy product (powdered milk), a legume (soy flour), grains (oats, wheat germ), seeds (sunflower, sesame) and nuts (almonds)—able to complement each other in different combinations.

BANANA PROTEIN DRINK

1 cup milk
4 tablespoons milk powder
1 banana
1 teaspoon cinnamon

Blend all ingredients in the blender. Makes one serving.

LUNCH

It should be no problem to plan a wide variety of nutritious lunches. There are homemade soups and whole-grain bread, salad, cheese or yogurt and fruit, raw vegetables and dip, smoothies (blender drinks), and sandwiches of all kinds.

Here are some sandwich possibilities:

1. Avocado with alfalfa sprouts, watercress, grated carrots
2. Nut loaf with lettuce and mayonnaise
3. Peanut butter with honey or raisins or bananas or granola
4. Cream cheese with fruit or cucumber or olives
5. Cottage cheese with celery or olives or chopped nuts
6. Mashed or pureed beans (like garbanzo) with celery or grated carrots and mayonnaise.

Vary the whole-grain bread. Also use buns or pita (pocket) bread. Alfalfa sprouts have protein value, are rich in vitamins and minerals, and are a source of energy. They are inexpensive and very easy to grow at home. Add them to sandwiches and salads.

SUNFLOWER BURGERS

1 cup ground sunflower seeds
¼ cup ground peanuts
½ cup shredded carrot
½ cup minced celery
1 tablespoon oil
¼ cup tomato sauce or juice, or
     vegetable cocktail
Herb seasoning to taste

Combine ingredients and mix well. Make patties and place on a lightly greased pan. Bake at 350 degrees, turning to brown on both sides. If desired, top with melted cheese.

The combination of sunflower seeds (seeds) and peanuts (legumes) makes a good source of protein.

BASIC SMOOTHIE

1 cup fruit juice
1 banana
Other fruit—a papaya, mango,
     orange, or berries
Honey or soft dates (to taste)

Blend in blender. Serves two.

DINNER

STEAMING VEGETABLES

An excellent way to cook vegetables is to steam them. This can be done in a stainless-steel steamer basket, over hot water, in a pan with a tight-fitting lid. Because you use much less water than you would when boiling vegetables, fewer nutrients and flavor are dissolved in the water. Cook vegetables for the *least* possible time necessary.

NOODLES AND VEGETABLES

Noodles—try Oriental type,
  if available
Tamari or other soy sauce (see note
  below)
Chopped vegetables—any
  combination of the following:
  carrots, bell pepper, broccoli,
  tomatoes, potato, cauliflower,
  mushrooms
Grated cheddar or Monterey Jack
  cheese

Boil noodles in water. Meanwhile, fill a pan about one-quarter full of water and put in vegetable steamer. First put in vegetables which need the most cooking, steam a little, then add the rest of the vegetables. Steam vegetables until just tender. Drain noodles and place in serving bowl. Mix noodles and tamari to taste. Add vegetables on top and sprinkle grated cheese over all.

Note: Tamari is a soy sauce. It is made with soybeans, wheat, and sea salt and is available in health food stores. Some soy sauces are mostly water and caramel coloring.

STIR-FRYING VEGETABLES

Stir-frying is the Oriental way to cook vegetables, done in an uncovered pan over a high heat. The vegetables are stirred continuously and for the shortest possible period, until they are tender-crisp.

ALMOND STIR-FRIED VEGETABLES WITH TOFU

Chopped vegetables—any
    combination of the following:
    carrots, celery, cauliflower,
    green beans, broccoli, zucchini,
    Chinese peas, bamboo shoots,
    water chestnuts, mushrooms
1 block tofu, cut in chunks (see note
    below)
Whole blanched almonds
Oil
Tamari or other soy sauce

Heat oil in a wok or heavy frying pan over medium-high heat. Lightly brown the tofu and almonds, remove with slotted spoon, and set aside. Put the vegetables that need longer cooking into the pan first, tossing them in the oil until they are coated. Stir-fry for about a minute, then add the vegetables that need less cooking time. Continue stirring for only a few more minutes, until the vegetables are almost crisp-tender. Add the tofu to the pan, and sprinkle tamari sauce over the mixture. Remove from heat, mix in the almonds, and serve immediately.

Note: Tofu is soybean curd. It is highly digestible, low in calories, entirely free of cholesterol, and high in protein and calcium, and it contains vitamins B_6, B_{12}, and E. It has a very mild taste itself and will take on the taste of whatever you mix it with. It's very versatile and is limited in use only by imagination. It can be used in soup, stew, casseroles, salad dressing, sandwiches, or even dessert.

NUT LOAF

2 tablespoons butter
2 stalks celery, chopped and lightly
    sautéed in the butter
1 carrot, grated
1 cup chopped walnuts
1 cup chopped cashews
½ cup ground peanuts
¼ cup ground sunflower seeds
½ cup rolled oats
1 lb. cottage cheese
1 block tofu, well-drained of liquid
    (optional)
2 eggs or egg replacer
½ teaspoon basil
½ teaspoon oregano

Mix all ingredients well. Put into a greased loaf pan and bake for approximately 1½ hours at 375 degrees.

Leftovers are excellent in sandwiches.

SPINACH LASAGNE

½ lb. cooked lasagne (whole wheat
    or spinach noodles)
2 bunches spinach, chopped, or 1
    package frozen chopped
    spinach
¼ lb. mushrooms
4 cups favorite tomato sauce
    (2 15-oz. cans or bottles)
¾ cup cottage cheese, or ricotta
¾ lb. mozzarella cheese

Steam spinach until tender. (Or defrost frozen spinach until it can be broken apart.) Cook lasagne until tender and drain. Brown mushrooms in oil, and add tomato sauce. (If adding spices to sauce, let it simmer.) In large roasting pan or casserole, arrange in layers: lasagne, spinach, cottage cheese, and mozzarella cheese. Cover with tomato sauce. Bake at 400 degrees for 45 minutes.

Carbohydrates are a dietary essential, crucial to the metabolic process that produces energy. Starches and sugars provide energy as glucose, or are stored as glycogen in the muscles and liver. For this reason, my pre-match meal is usually pasta—preferably spaghetti.

SWEET AND SOUR SAUCE

½ cup pineapple juice (reserve
    pineapple chunks)
3 tablespoons oil
2 tablespoons honey
1 teaspoon soy sauce
½ teaspoon pepper
¼ cup mild vinegar

Heat above ingredients, then thicken with arrowroot. Add pineapple chunks. Serve over stir-fried steamed vegetables and brown rice.

BROWN GRAVY

2 tablespoons whole wheat flour
2 tablespoons oil
2 teaspoons tamari or other soy
    sauce
1 cup vegetable broth (can be made
    with water and broth seasoning)

Mix flour, oil, and tamari over low flame. Stir vegetable broth into the mixture, and continue stirring until gravy is smooth.

This gravy is good on nut loaf and sunflower burgers.

MUSHROOM SAUCE

2 cups mushrooms, sliced
3 tablespoons butter
3 tablespoons flour
1½ cups milk
Salt, pepper, tamari to taste

Fry mushrooms in butter until soft. Add flour and stir to coat mushrooms. Stir in milk and seasoning to taste. Stir frequently over low heat until sauce thickens.

Good in casseroles, over whole-wheat noodles, or on Nut Loaf.

ENERGY BARS

1 cup carob powder (see note below)
1 cup milk powder (try soy milk
    powder if available)
1 cup honey
½ cup margarine
½ cup oil
1 teaspoon vanilla
Pinch of salt
½ cup cashews
½ cup sesame seeds
½ cup sunflower seeds
½ cup raisins

Cream oil, margarine, honey, vanilla, and salt until smooth. Add carob and milk powders and mix well. Stir in remaining ingredients. Press into flat pan. Chill to harden. Cut into squares.

Note: Carob powder is made from pods of the carob tree. It is a source of calcium, phosphorus, potassium, and iron, is low in fat, and lacks the caffeinlike stimulant of chocolate.

BANANA YOGURT PIE

Crust:
1/3 cup rolled oats
1/4 cup walnuts, chopped
1/4 cup raisins
1/4 cup dates, chopped
2 tablespoons oil or melted butter

Mix together. (Add a little water if needed for ingredients to stick together.) Press into a pie plate. Bake about 10 minutes at 250 degrees.

Filling:
2/3 cup yogurt
8 oz. cream cheese, soft
1 teaspoon vanilla
2 tablespoons honey
Bananas
Shredded coconut

Beat together the cream cheese, yogurt, vanilla, and honey until smooth. Line bottom of pie shell with banana slices. Pour yogurt mixture over top. Refrigerate several hours or overnight before serving. (Variation: Use blueberries instead of bananas.)

If you served a light dinner, or one without much protein, a dessert like this pie, with yogurt, cream cheese, and nuts, will round out the meal.

196